JFK
Profile in Literature

Klaus A. Uellenberg

JFK
Profile in Literature

PETER LANG
EDITION

Bibliographic Information published by the Deutsche Nationalbibliothek
The Deutsche Nationalbibliothek lists this publication in the Deutsche Nationalbibliografie; detailed bibliographic data is available in the internet at http://dnb.d-nb.de.

Library of Congress Cataloging-in-Publication Data

Uellenberg, Klaus A.
JFK : Profile in Literature / Klaus A. Uellenberg.
pages cm
Includes bibliographical references.
ISBN 978-3-631-64328-0
1. Kennedy, John F. (John Fitzgerald), 1917-1963—In literature.
2. American literature—20th century—History and criticism.
3. Collective memory in literature. I. Title.
PS225.U38 2013
810.9'355—dc23
2013017518

Cover photo: "Kennedy sailing off coast of Maine 1962" – Robert Knudsen, White House / John F. Kennedy Presidential Library, Boston.

ISBN 978-3-631-64328-0 (Print)
E-ISBN 978-3-653-03314-4 (E-Book)
DOI 10.3726/978-3-653-03314-4

Peter Lang Edition is an Imprint of Peter Lang GmbH.

Peter Lang – Frankfurt am Main · Bern · Bruxelles · New York · Oxford · Warszawa · Wien

www.peterlang.de

The great enemy of the truth is very often not the
deliberate, contrived, and dishonest –
but the myth – persistent, persuasive, and unrealistic.

John F. Kennedy,
New Haven,
June 11, 1962

For
Kristin

Contents

Introduction

John F. Kennedy earns top ranking among America's presidents in the estimation of his fellow countrymen. Asked in 1975 to name the greatest president most Americans chose him.[1] A similar survey in 1983 concluded that "Kennedy has become America's favorite president."[2] In 1996 most of those polled wished that he were president.[3] And when asked in 2008 "of all the presidents America has ever had, who would you want most to be the next president?" their choice was John Kennedy.[4]

There are, however, other appraisals. When historians, political scientists and lawyers were requested in 1982 and 2000 to award the presidents one of the five grades "great", "near great", "above average", "below average" or "failure", they rated Kennedy "above average", putting him in13th and 8th place respectively.[5] A 2009 ranking by historians placed him sixth.[6] In point of fact these surveys are of limited value for distinguishing accomplishment, if alone due to the lack of a valid basis for comparison. Such assessments involve examining the outcomes from terms of office of very different lengths (1037 days for Kennedy, 12 years for Franklin D. Roosevelt) and highly differing historical and political circumstances and leadership challenges. It nevertheless remains beyond dispute that Kennedy is not accorded the prime position he wins from the public at large.

But it is not only public opinion vs. professional and journalistic rating that differs. Divergent views also compete with each other within the body of research work on Kennedy. As briefly outlined below, his upbringing, his personality and his political record and its impacts are discussed controversially.

Kennedy's youth is time and again overshadowed by sickness affecting his physical development. Persistently underweight, he is so gaunt at the age of fourteen that his classmates call him "rat face". He struggles in striving for academic and athletic success, unlike his older brother, Joe Jr., who is often compared to him more favorably, and he has difficulty meeting the expectations of his extremely ambitious father. Confronted with such challenges in his formative years he is said to have developed a strongly independent and self-assertive personality, along with "a profound sense of life's limitations"[7].

At the same time, according to this view, he acquired empathy for the needs of others, as well as self-irony and self-criticism. The long hours confined to bed with illness and devoted to reading, above all about history, contributed to his intellectual development and laid the foundation for his deep interest in historical and political issues. Thanks to a love of books he was exposed to a wealth of ideas, opinions, personal histories and political topics, including many related contradictions and complexities which roused his reasoning abilities and his intellectual curiosity early on. These character traits would later cause him to seek out the company of intellectuals and artists, and to award them a place of honor in public life. Dealing with personal adversity also helped him cultivate the strength and determination to confront challenges and tackle problems. This was accompanied by an exceptional presence of mind which served as the source of his coolheadedness, steering him away from ideological fervor and towards pragmatism and rational posturing.

In foreign policy he wins greatest acclaim for the de-escalation of the Cold War and a renunciation of the arms race. As the East-West Conflict culminated in the Cuban Missile Crisis, the most dangerous face-off in history, he made the decision to impose a naval blockade against the placement of missiles on Cuba. In a display of "wise statesmanship"[8] he level-headedly maneuvered between the alternatives of atomic extortion by the Russians on the one hand and the armed intervention preferred by the American military and many of his civilian advisors on the other, a course of action which we know today, in all probability, would have resulted in an atomic war. Ratification of the Nuclear Test Ban Treaty initiated by him, and his success in reshaping NATO doctrine from a policy of massive retaliation to one of flexible response were instrumental in replacing prescribed nuclear escalation with less perfunctory alternatives for reacting in cases of conflict. This led to the end of nuclear diplomacy, the reduced threat of nuclear war and the pursuit of détente politics – the essentials of a "peaceful and prudent foreign policy."[9] In a 2007 feature titled "How to lead in a dangerous world"[10] *Time* magazine called his statesmanship exemplary and honored him as a "warrior for peace"[11].

Assessments of his domestic policies have likewise concluded that he was very successful.[12] He contributed to narrowing the gap of disparity in American society, notably between the rich and the poor with his "War on Poverty", and between African Americans and whites with his advocacy for civil rights. Praised alongside these social measures are his successful, partially interventionist economic and fiscal policies, which included Keynesian-inspired tax reductions to spur growth, along with measures to combat unemployment. He wins further approval for upgrading the nation's infrastructure, including revitalization programs for large, problem-ridden cities and improvements to the quality of education, social welfare and health insurance. Hindered with a strongly oppositional Congress dominated by conservatives, he had limited maneuverability in putting his ambitious agenda into practice which made cautiously safeguarding legislative initiatives a necessity. At the same time, he promoted a full array of decisive social reforms and anchored them so solidly in the legislative process that – like his Civil Rights Program – they were passed by Congress after his death: "He planted many seedlings, but lived only long enough to see some flower."[13]

His presidency reflected a pragmatic idealism lacking delusion, rational analysis rather than ideological positioning, and "the ability to compromise on tactics without compromising principles."[14] Numerous lasting and far reaching steps were initiated which, had he not fallen victim to his assassin(s), could have been completed – "it was […] as if Lincoln had been killed six months after Gettysburg or Franklin Roosevelt at the end of 1935 or Truman before the Marshall Plan."[15]

This version of events is not unanimously accepted. Some critics argue that Kennedy was raised in an "emotional wasteland"[16], materially privileged but emotionally deprived. He appeared neglected by a reserved, detached and often absent mother and an even more frequently absent and strange father[17] who, oblivious to his son's weak physical condition, consistently expected top performance nonetheless. Mercilessly taunted by his older brother and later sent away to a series of boarding schools, he was conditioned early on to having his emotional needs ignored. From this experience he allegedly developed an even greater need for attention, but also heartlessness. This, combined with the role model of his notoriously promiscuous father, turned him into an infamous womanizer. His weak health and the dominance of his brother had the effect of undermining his masculine identity.[18] In order to compensate for this he was prone to proving his competitiveness, manliness and virility, which to Gary Wills made him appear on the political stage as a "macho president"[19] whose foreign policy Bruce Mazlish accordingly sees rooted in "a virile anticommunism"[20]. The result was unnecessarily aggressive and confrontational behavior such as that exhibited during the Cuban Missile Crisis. In general he is found to have conformed to the Cold War consensus, with actions that were conservative in nature and lacking in inspiration. He is further accused of overestimating his own capabilities, for instance with his program for reform and democratization in Latin America, the Alliance for Progress, which did not achieve its full potential during the thousand days of his prematurely terminated presidency.

Domestically he is viewed as having breached only a limited number of important legislative impasses because his behavior was largely reactive rather than proactive. Cited as an example is the Civil Rights Act, which he proposed but which was ratified only after his death. Other critics accuse his presidency of having had more style than substance. He himself, they maintain, merely projected a deceivingly artificial image, "a product,"[21] shaped and embellished by clever public relations management. This included a "myth-making machine"[22] of speech writers, submissive journalists and intellectual elites, all blinded by his wealth and his aura of splendor, which acted on them like opium;[23] "a captivated (indeed, some might say, captive) press corps pitched in to enthusiastically limn the mythology: gloss and class."[24] These observers concede him his intelligence, wit, charm and charisma. They also acknowledge him to have been "politically experienced, eager for information, respectful of first-class minds, and willing to link the presidency with good taste and high culture."[25] But they also charge him with applying these qualities in a tactical manner to manipulate others. His coolness and composure are merely considered superficial manifestations of a lack of deep moral conviction and personal commitment.[26] Sophistication and style are reduced to the level of performance. Intellectualism and his patronage of the arts and literature are interpreted as empty posturing, the product of an adroit image campaign for a president whose favorite reading material typically included Ian Fleming's novels about James Bond, "the debonair, womanizing, rule-breaking, cold warrior."[27]

Given his overall high public approval rating, this revisionist viewpoint[28] appears to carry less weight than the more positive assessment for ordinary American citizens in forming their verdict of Kennedy. All the same, both views of Kennedy continue to co-exist as competing images outside the realm of literature. How literary texts approach the matter, that is to say which of the contradictory versions they choose to espouse and what contributions they make to the perception of Kennedy, has not yet been systematically examined. This is despite the fact that a body of such literary work has been generated over the last five decades significant enough in size to warrant attention. It is this shortcoming that this book addresses. To date only two unrelated publications have appeared, an article in an academic journal[29] and one chapter in a book[30], but they do not deal with formal analyses which are the basis of this study.

Kennedy provides subject matter for plays, poetry and a variety of narratives. As might be expected, the forms of treatment differ, each employing a particular approach to him which opens perspectives and reveals insights. In what follows, the specifics of these works are examined in separate analyses; the results of these findings are then synthesized into a concluding synchronic overview. Serving as the central core are the narratives, which form a homogeneous body of text due to their comparability. The other genres are considered thereafter.

The concept of collective memory serves here as a key frame of reference. This heuristic tool, developed from the theories of the philosopher and sociologist Maurice Halbwachs and the cultural theorist Aby Warburg, constitutes the collective acts of sharing and symbolically (re)constructing distinct knowledge of the past. The organic process attributed to individual memory is metaphorically transferred to a group as a whole. However,

> it must [...] be emphatically clarified that such entities do not *have* a collective memory, but rather *form* one with the help of many types of symbolic media such as texts, pictures, memorials, anniversaries and commemorative rituals.[31]

Collective memory conserves the pool of mutually revered past remembrances of a select group of people, in this case U.S. Americans. It mirrors the group itself and is, like its members, characterized by diversity and continual transformation. The construct smoothly transitions with the broader notion of historical consciousness. The concept of collective memory is useful in two ways for the purposes of this book. Firstly, it serves as a repository for both the real and the imaginary – a "vessel of codified knowledge across time and space"[32] – and furnishes a framework for comprehensively organizing the distinct aspects of Kennedy gleaned from the individual texts. Secondly, it offers a progressive means of accessing the special role Kennedy plays in the American mind. Given the transdisciplinary scope of this study, drawing upon such fields as literature, history, psychology and sociology, it provides a suitable approach to Kennedy from a literary perspective within a cultural studies context.

Collective memory manifests itself in acts of remembrance which are linked to media of group recollections that avail themselves to observation and analysis. In the case of Kennedy these media comprise non-fictional texts (historical or journalistic writings, for example), surveys, the establishment and operating of the JFK Presidential Library, the naming of buildings and institutions after him (John F. Kennedy Airport, the John F. Kennedy School of Government at Harvard University, the Kennedy Space Center, the John F. Kennedy Center for the Performing Arts, etc.), as well as memorial celebrations, and literature. The latter in particular deserves special attention because

> literary texts create fictional worlds and, by being able to present memory through diverse forms of representation, literature plays an important role in the formation of collective memory, a role which non-fictional texts cannot replicate.[33]

With respect to literature's specific contribution, the questions dealt with in this book are: How is John Kennedy envisioned in and through American literature? Do the analyses of the individual works generate a coherent or an elusive literary profile? What conclusions can be drawn concerning Kennedy's status in America's collective memory? Can any generalized assertions be made about literature's treatment of him?

Remembering takes its orientation and structure from time and space as the coordinates of life. The three successive perspectives of Kennedy which comprise the main body of this work derive from these dimensions. The first section covers the assassination in Dallas, Texas with Don DeLillo's *Libra* and Richard Brautigan's *The Tokyo-Montana Express* as key postmodern works, along with their counterparts in the traditional vein, John Updike's *Couples*, Wright Morris' *One Day* and William Manchester's *The Death of a President,* among others. The second part deals with the presidential years in Washington D.C. with William F. Buckley's *See You Later Alligator* and Norman Mailer's *Harlot's*

Ghost. The third section focuses on the early years in and around Boston with Anton Myrer's *The Last Convertible* and Vance Bourjaily's *The man who knew Kennedy*. The book concludes by turning attention to Barbara Garson's drama *MacBird!*, Wendy McLeod's play *The House of Yes* and a number of poems.

Dallas

> At the airport they were standing on baggage carts and clinging to light posts. They were draped over the chain-link fence, people in raincoats, waving flags, hanging off the sign for gate 28. Skies were clear now and the 707 swung massively to a stop on the tarmac. They came running from their cars. They stood at the edge of the crowd, jumping up and down. Children rode the shoulders of gangly men. There was a mood rising from the packed bodies, an eager spirit of assent. Members of the welcoming party edged into place at the foot of the ramp, fussing with their clothes and hair. The aft door opened and the First Lady appeared in a glow of rosebud pink, suit and hat to match, followed by the President. A sound, an awe worked through the crowd, a recognition, ringing in the air. People called out together, faces caught in some stage of surprise, resembling dazzled pain. "Here" or "Jack" or "Look." The President fingered his lapel, gave a little jacket-adjusting shrug and walked down the ramp. The sound was a small roar now, a wonder. They shook the fence. They came running from the terminal building, handbags and cameras bouncing. There were cameras everywhere, held aloft, a rustling of bladed shutters, with homemade signs poking through the mass.
>
> Welcome Jack and Jackie to Big D.
>
> After the handshakes and salutes, Jack Kennedy walked away from his security, sidestepping puddles, and went to the fence. He reached a hand into the ranks and they surged forward, looking at each other to match reactions. He moved along the fence, handsome and tanned, smiling famously into the wall of open mouths. He looked like himself, like photographs, a helmsman squinting in the seaglare, white teeth shinning. There was only a trace of cortisone bloat that sometimes affected his face – cortisone for his Addison's disease, a back brace for his degenerating discs. They came over the fence surrounding him, so many people and hands.[34]

The President is receiving a rousing welcome at Love Field Airport. In his novel *Libra* Don DeLillo depicts this tense scene of heightened expectation with descriptions that adhere closely to photographs and film clips of the historic event. But the account, which comes at the very beginning of a chapter in his book about November 22, 1963, contains perceptive contrasts that already cloud the picture. The anonymous nature of "they" is emphasized through anaphora and juxtaposed with phrases such as "packed bodies", "the mass" or "wall of open mouths" to highlight the distinction between the faceless crowd and the recognizable and well known Kennedy. His outward appearance ("handsome and tanned", "like photographs, a helmsman squinting into the seaglare – white teeth shining"), in turn, contradicts his physique ("Addison's disease", "degenerating discs"). These contrasts work to tone down the euphoric mood of the reception.

Kennedy is treading on uncertain ground by coming to Dallas, a city considered to be a potentially dangerous campaign stopover for him. There are posters around town bearing his picture along with accusations of high treason. His conciliatory pursuit of de-escalation with Havana and Moscow and, more importantly, his support for African Americans in their struggle for equal civil rights, have caused Southern whites to turn against him. When UN Ambassador Adlai Stevenson arrived in town as a Kennedy Administration representative one month earlier, he was spit upon and struck with a picket sign. *US News and World Report* wrote "Even the word 'Kennedy' is an epithet in some parts of the South."[35] But even if Kennedy could no longer count on winning a majority of the southern vote in the upcoming 1964 presidential election, his campaign was not ready to completely forfeit Florida and Texas. Consequently, these two heavily populated states were tacked on to his travel itinerary through a number of states out west. The chief purpose of the trip was to raise campaign funds and help ease tensions within the Texas Democratic Party.

In DeLillo's novel, as in actuality, the enthusiastic reception does not cause Kennedy to forget the realities of Dallas: "We're heading into nut county now" (393), he whispers to his wife in the open blue Lincoln as the motorcade begins the drive into the city.

Compositionally, the events in Dallas constitute a vanishing point in the novel where three plot strands converge: a conspiracy to kill the president, a biographical sketch of Oswald and, with somewhat of a time delay, an attempt to tell the story of the assassination and the events leading up to it.

In the first narrative line, CIA veteran Win Everett devises a plan to redeem America from its defeat at the Bay of Pigs with a group of co-conspirators including Lawrence Parmeter, Guy Banister and a number of other Castro opponents, some with ties to the Mafia. Everett had taken part in the Bay of Pigs fiasco, was dismissed at the time from active service and is now seeking to revamp his own past along with that of the nation. Fearing that Kennedy might resolve the Cuba conflict peacefully, Everett sees a pressing need for action:

> If we want a second invasion, a full-bore attempt this time, without restrictions or conditions, we have to do something soon. We have to move the Cuban matter past the edge of all these sweet maneuverings. We need an event that will excite and shock the exile community, the whole country. (27)

His thinking is that "we want to set up an attempt on the life of the President" (27). The attempt shall fail, but a trail shall remain leading back to Cuba to serve as the *casus belli* for a justified American invasion of the island to ouster Castro: "Of course Everett did not plan to shoot Kennedy in the strict sense. Only to lay down fire in the street. He wanted a surgical miss" (219). He suggests:

> [We] leave a dim trail. The evidence is ambiguous. But it points to the Cuban Intelligence Directorate. Inherent in the plan is a second set of clues, even more unclear, more intriguing. They point to the Agency's attempt to assassinate Castro. I'm designing a plan that includes

> elements of both the American provocation and the Cuban reply. We do the whole thing with paper. Passports, drivers' licenses, address books. Our team of shooters disappears but the police find a trail. Mail order forms, change-of-address cards, photographs. We script a person out of ordinary pocket litter. (27-28)

Their intention is for investigators to construe a scenario from contrived evidence and confusing clues which, except for the link to Cuba and a yet to be named scapegoat, can only be traced back to pure happenstance. Everett's strategy is: "Create coincidences so bizarre, they have to believe it" (147). He initially also conjures up an imaginary figure to be the assassin:

> He [Everett] felt marvelously alert, sure of himself, putting together a man with scissors and tape.
>
> His gunman would emerge and vanish in a maze of false names. Investigators would find an application card for a post-office box; a certificate of service, U.S. Marine Corps; a Social Security Card; a passport application; a driver's license; a stolen credit card and half a dozen other documents – in two or three different names. (145-6)

Later on, Lee Harvey Oswald is manipulated into this role. He becomes a sacrificial pawn as Everett's plan takes on a life of its own and turns into an actual presidential murder as the only way to ensure an unavoidable war with Cuba. As for Oswald, "his role was to provide artifacts of historical interest, a traceable weapon, all the cuttings and hoardings of his Cuban career" (386).

The novel's second plot strand chronicles Oswald's short life: an unsettled and difficult childhood in the Bronx and New Orleans, undistinguished service with the Marine Corps in Japan, a brief interlude of defection to the Soviet Union and marriage to a Russian, work for the pro-Castro Fair Play for Cuba Committee back in New Orleans, visits to the Cuban and Soviet embassies in Mexico just weeks before the assassination, and finally the shooting in Dallas and his own murder and funeral.

In an interview with novelist Anne Tyler DeLillo states, "I tried to stay as close to what I understood to be the actual Oswald as I could."[36] In separate interviews he stresses the importance of factuality for him: "I really didn't take liberty with fact so much as I invented fresh fact."[37]

What ensues is the personal history of a loner and an outsider, a man incapable of maintaining balance in his life despite being born under the zodiac sign of the scale, the astrological reference that is the novel's title. DeLillo brings up Oswald's dyslexia repeatedly, suggesting that the problems he has recognizing words also prevent him in a broader context from properly "reading" or sizing up real life situations. Over and over again he reveals himself to be insecure when sorting out his experiences and in distinguishing between important and inconsequential matters:

> The next day – it was September 9 – Lee picked up the *Times-Picayune* and read that Castro was charging the U.S. with plotting assassinations.

> […] Lee read the story several times. It was as if they had control of the news, Ferrie, Banister, all of them, all-knowing. Of course it was only coincidence that Ferrie mentioned the thing one day and it appeared in the paper the next. But maybe that was even stranger than total control.
>
> Coincidence. He learned in the bayous, from Raymo, that Castro's guerrilla name was Alex, derived from his middle name, Alejandro. Lee used to be known as Alek.
>
> Coincidence. Banister was trying to find him, not knowing what city or state or county he was in, and he walked in the door at 544 and asked for an undercover job.
>
> Coincidence. He ordered the revolver and the carbine six weeks apart. They arrived the same day.
>
> Coincidence. Lee was always reading two or three books, like Kennedy. Did military service in the Pacific, like Kennedy. Poor handwriting, terrible speller, like Kennedy. Wives pregnant at the same time. Brothers named Robert. (336)

The precariousness of his circumstances, his shallow personality, his Marxist sympathies and his poor fit in American society stemming from his earlier defection to the Soviet Union, are factors that make it easy for the conspirators to turn him into their patsy. The final item on this list is his job at the School Book Depository on Elm Street, along the route in Dallas planned for the presidential motorcade.

Up on the sixth floor Oswald awaits the approaching open limousine unaware of the other, actual marksmen: "as a shooter, Oswald was redundant, strictly backup" (386). As the cheering of the crowd continues along the street below, Kennedy moves into target position. Oswald sights him from the rear, the other conspirators from a grassy knoll ahead of Kennedy's car on the right. The first shot pierces his throat; the second one hits Governor Connelly, seated in front on the same side of the car, "then the third shot sent stuff just everywhere. Tissue, bone fragments, tissue in pale wads, watery mess, tissue, blood, brain matter all over them" (399).

In the third narrative line the job of analyzing the assassination evidence and writing up a secret murder report for the CIA falls to semi-retired agent Nicholas Branch. He becomes increasingly overwhelmed when the growing volume of data shows no signs of tapering off. He also suspects that certain material is being provided to him only reluctantly or perhaps not at all. Eventually he comes to feel incapable of organizing the myriad and disparate details into any sort of coherent story "because the data keeps coming in. Because new lives enter the record all the time. The past is changing as he writes" (301). Although he manages to identify a few patterns, he has difficulty distinguishing between the facts that are important and those that are merely incidental. The conspiracy thus comes full circle. Everett's motto for his plan of action is: "Leave them with coincidence, lingering mystery. This is what makes it real." (147) And Branch concludes, "there is enough mystery in the facts as we know them, enough conspiracy, coincidence, loose ends, dead ends, multiple interpretations" (58). In defeat he realizes that integrating all of the innumerable loose ends into his report is hopeless. The quantity of fragmented data has become so huge and so unruly that tying it all together in one complete and coherent account is simply not possible:

> He has learned enough about the days and months preceeding November 22, and enough about the twenty-second itself, to reach a determination that the conspiracy against the President was a rambling affair that succeeded in the short term due mainly to chance. Deft men and fools, ambivalence and fixed will and what the weather was like. (441)

Perpetrators, premeditation, ambivalence and chance have all colluded to prevent any meaningful conclusions from rising to the surface.

At this point the novel advances to a metafictional and metahistorical level where the attempt to write the story of the Kennedy assassination is set down in a self-reflexive manner. This effort ultimately ends in defeat. What is unexplained becomes unexplainable. In the process *Libra* comes to undermine not just itself as a conspiracy theory, but all other conspiracy theories as well. Importantly, DeLillo claims all the same that his version of the assassination is the most plausible:

> My own feeling at the very beginning was that I had to do justice to historical likelihood. In other words, I chose what I consider the most obvious possibility: that the assassination was the work of anti-Castro elements.[38]

The contradiction expressed in DeLillo's twisted positioning here illustrates a characteristic of postmodernism referred to as "paradoxical identity" by Linda Hutcheon in *A Poetics of Postmodernism*.[39] She comments on this concept as follows:

> While unresolved paradoxes may be unsatisfying to those in need of absolute and final answers, to postmodernist thinkers and artists they have been the source of intellectual energy that has provoked new articulations of the postmodern condition.[40]

Libra can thus be understood as a postmodern metaconspiracy presenting its own theory of the Kennedy assassination and simultaneously excluding the possibility of a historiographical master explanation ever existing to bring the speculation surrounding Kennedy's death to an end. The book depicts the case as one that will never be rationally solved because of machinations which remain obscure or, as DeLillo puts it in the novel, "too many people, too many levels of plotting" (304). Within the realm of imagination, however, he nevertheless attempts to rise to the challenge and provide answers to the unresolved questions of who, how and why. He simply dispenses with the need or ability to rationally explain coincidental happenstances such as those conceived by Everett and uncovered by Branch. The result is a repeated emphasis on coincidence which, as Glen Thomas points out, lends the narrative some similarity to a chaos theory of history.[41]

As a postmodern conspiracy narrative *Libra* clearly distinguishes itself from other conspiracy novels about the Kennedy assassination. These thrillers tend to focus on how secret service agents, politicians, businessmen or members of organized crime manage to pull off the murder. In Robert Littell's *The Sisters* CIA affiliates activate a Russian "sleeper agent" to do the killing with the help of his Soviet case officer who is smuggled into the U.S. William F. Buckley bases the plot of *Mongoose, R.I.P.* on Cuban retaliation for CIA actions against Castro, the same context used by James Ellroy in *American Tabloid*. Charles McCarry in *The Tears of Autumn* explores Kennedy's death as an act of revenge for the 1963 CIA coup against Viet Nam's dictatorial leader Ngo Dinh Diem. In *Winter Kills* Richard Condons sets the assassination against the backdrop of a conflict between the Mafia and Joseph P. Kennedy Sr. Compared to these and other similar narratives, DeLillo's *Libra* is a novel of far greater depth. He uses Oswald, for example, to illustrate his views of manipulation and subjugation of the individual. He likewise turns Branch's failed attempt to produce the CIA report into a paradigm for the notion that it is generally impossible to write any authoritative history. This postmodern view of historiography as mere construct is one that DeLillo shares with other contemporaries, including John Barth, Thomas Pynchon and Tim O'Brien.

In *Libra* he combines this view with a postmodern textuality, one he achieves by mixing such diverse elements as fictional conspiracy theory, factual biography, and metafiction. The conventional boundaries for defining categories of classification dissolve with his use of this strategy and, as a result, the destructive events of Dallas are replicated in a corresponding dissolution in his novel at the textual level as well.

As a postmodern metaconspiracy *Libra* calls into question conspiracy theories fashioned not only as fiction, but also as non-fiction. The number of these theories in circulation has steadily multiplied ever since the assassination occurred. Even before the US government released its official report by the investigation commission under Chief Justice Earl Warren in September 1964, the media had begun casting doubts about its findings. The Warren Report, as it has come to be known, runs 888 pages in length with 26 volumes of supplemental exhibits and testimony. Its total length of roughly 17,000 pages notwithstanding, the report generated immediate and controversial accusations of inadequate research, incompleteness and lack of coherence. The untimely deaths of some key witnesses raised further doubts about its findings. Robert Kennedy privately dismissed it as a "shoddy piece of craftsmanship."[42] A great many alternate scenarios and attempts to uncover the truth have surfaced since its publication the year following the murder. Critics have chiefly focused on the commission's conclusion that Oswald was the sole assassin and his lack of a motive. Most skeptics point to evidence indicating that Kennedy died in crossfire coming from more than one marksman, or in other words as the result of collusion.

The plethora of differing theories published and debated in the media in the years after the murder eventually prompted the journalist Jacob Brackman to instigate a hoax in 1967. Writing in the political and literary journal *Ramparts* he discussed a work called *Time of the Assassins* by one Ulov G.K. LeBoeuf, who professed that the deaths of Marylin Monroe, John F. Kennedy and Aldous Huxley were all related to one another. In reality no such book was ever published. Brackman subsequently explained in an article in the *New Yorker* that the purpose of the fake review was to motivate readers to seek out the truth. As a put-on artist he claimed to hope "that people, when their legs have been pulled almost to the breaking point, will at last begin to kick."[43]

Barbie Zelizer contends that during the decade which followed, in view of "Vietnam, Watergate, and other scandals of the seventies [...] questioning the assassination record [...] had its roots in larger cultural and political enterprises that cast doubt on governmental institutions and recognized forms of documentation."[44] Growing public pressure eventually led to the creation of a House Select Committee on Assassinations in 1976 to examine the deaths of both John F. Kennedy and Martin Luther King. The conclusion in its report published two years later was blatant: "The Warren Commission failed to investigate adequately the possibility of a conspiracy to assassinate the President."[45] Even taking into account that certain critical information was lacking in the immediate aftermath of the murder, for example knowledge kept secret about CIA and Mafia cooperation in attempts on the life of Castro, the Warren Report was judged to have failed to do justice to the evidential findings and discoveries that were available, in particular with regard to possible collusion.[46] The House Select Committee surmised "that President Kennedy was probably assassinated as a result of a conspiracy."[47] Potential motives are attributed to the Cuban government, the Soviets, Cuban exiles, the CIA, the FBI, the Secret Service and, in particular, organized crime. The report highlights the "violent attitude of powerful organized crime figures toward the President and Attorney General Robert Kennedy, their capacity to commit murder, including assassination, and their possible access to Oswald through his associates or relatives."[48] This correlates with investigative findings "that the Kennedy administration brought about the strongest effort against organized crime that had ever been coordinated by the Federal Government."[49]

But for the critics, even this investigation failed to go far enough to draw a definitive conclusion. "While it had displaced the Warren commission's lone gunman theory with notions of conspiracy, the committee had not lent closure to the story" according to Zelizer.[50] To this day the theory mill continues to turn, in recent years with the added support of access to the previously unavailable documents released under the President John F. Kennedy Assassination Records Act of 1992. Stephen King's novel *11.22.63* published in 2011, for example, returns to the theory of Oswald as the sole assassin.[51]

Analyzing and evaluating the many rivaling and at times overlapping accounts has evolved into an unending investigative process. Newer technology-based procedures in the fields of forensics, ballistics, ultrasound and film analysis, details heretofore left unexplored, newly voiced testimonies and other more recently uncovered information all serve to furnish these efforts with continued momentum and, occasionally, to substantiate decades old speculations with fresh evidence.

Many conspiracy theorists, in contrast to the Warren Commission, rest their arguments on the *cui bono* principle which correlates accountability for an act with attaining some definable goal. There are many differing conclusions. Some theories remain focused on the CIA and anti-Castro forces, as in *Libra*, while others continue to look toward organized crime or the Castro regime. An alternative theory involving the influential power and lucrative business dealings of the American military-industrial complex gained wide public attention from Oliver Stone's award-winning but controversial film *JFK,* released in 1991. Other evidence points to conservative factions with a possible link to Texan oil money. These groups may have had an interest in crippling Kennedy's diplomacy of détente or blocking further advances in the field of civil rights. These same motives underpin allegations of an undercover coup by government agencies such as the CIA, combined with a fear that Kennedy's program of change might institute greater personal restrictions, loss of status and tighter public controls. Suspicions have been cast as far afield as the Federal Reserve, whose powerful, semi-autonomous status as central bank Kennedy attempted to rein in with an executive order in early June 1963. In still other theories Lyndon Johnson is accused of being either a criminal partner or a principal contractor to the murder. These theories hold that Johnson was either exploited as an accomplice by conspirators expecting favors from him once he got to the White House, or else he instigated the murder himself to satisfy his power lust for the presidency. That he contributed to some covering up and confusion during the murder investigation lends credence to these contentions. He may, however, have actually been trying to strengthen the lone gunman theory with Oswald as the marksman in order to preempt the threat of war were a communist conspiracy plot to come to light.

The following two prominent but expressly contradictory testimonials aptly illustrate how convoluted the investigative inquiry has become. Oscar Marino, who in 1963 was a leading member of Cuba's foreign secret service, asserted in 2006 that he had sound knowledge Kennedy was the victim of a Cuban murder contract carried out by Oswald.[52] The former chief counsel of the House Select Committee and leading organized crime expert G. Robert Blakey claimed in 1981 that he had solid evidence that Carlos Marcello, head of the New Orleans Mafia at the time, was the mastermind behind the assassination plot as personal revenge for his arrest and deportation to Guatemala in 1961 at the Kennedys' behest.[53]

Despite their claims to non-fiction, all of these conspiracy theories actually mix fiction with fact. This is because no distinct dividing line separates the two in the absence of a definitive account of the crime. "From the beginning the assassination record lacked closure. Characterized by incompleteness and incongruities, it drew groups trying to put forward competitively their authoritative views of what had happened."[54] By 1993 alone there were estimated to be roughly two thousand on the subject.[55] Interpretations abound. These very aspects of the assassination file – fragmentation, the absence of closure, blending (short-circuiting) fact and fiction, and the proliferation of meaning – are themselves postmodern attributes. Correspondingly there is a postmodern mindset to be found in the file with regard to fundamental manipulation, subordination, heteronomy, and non-transparency of the like that can be found in the literature of DeLillo and some of his contemporaries including the novels of Thomas Pynchon, in particular *The Crying of Lot 49* and *Vineland*.

These postmodern phenomena along with the many literary treatments of conspiracy which have emerged have also been materially influenced by the sequence of unsettling events which followed Kennedy's assassination. These span the murders of his brother Robert and Martin Luther King Jr., the Watergate scandal and the 9/11 terror attacks at the beginning of the current century. In *Postmodern Fiction* Larry McCaffery therefore convincingly singles out the day of Kennedy's death as "the day postmodernism was officially ushered in – at least in the United States – since that was the day that symbolically signaled the end of a certain kind of optimism and naivete in our collective consciousness, the end of certain verities and assurances."[56] The emergence of some postmodern characteristics from within and against modernism and from the postwar literature of the 1950s forms a complementary line of development.

The connection between Kennedy's death and the emergence of the new consciousness is described by DeLillo in his *Rolling Stone*-essay "American Blood":

> What has become unraveled since that afternoon in Dallas is not the plot, of course, [...] but the sense of a coherent reality most of us shared. We seem from that moment to have entered a world of randomness and ambiguity.[57]

The day of Kennedy's death has come to represent a cultural caesura for the United States, the starting point for a postmodern perception of reality. The significance of November 22, 1963 for American postmodernism sheds light, for example, on why DeLillo returns to the assassination again and again in his writing. It is a theme which runs through his novels *Americana, Players, Running Dog, Libra and Underworld*. His manner of critically protesting the way American reality was transformed that day is already typified in the main character of his very first novel, *Americana*. His protagonist drives through downtown Dallas following the route of Kennedy and his entourage of limousines while honking the horn. This act itself is an expression of the "postmodern condition":

> In the morning I headed west along Main Street in downtown Dallas. I turned right at Houston Street, turned left into Elm and pressed my hand against the horn. I kept it there as I drove past the School Book Depository, through Dealey Plaza and beneath the triple underpass. I kept blowing the horn all along Stemmons Freeway and out past Parkland Hospital.[58]

The death in Dallas is treated in a different postmodern way by Richard Brautigan in *The Tokyo-Montana Express*. The book is a collection of 131 fictional texts which trace an imaginary train line. In the part titled "What are you going to do with 390 photographs of Christmas trees?" the narrator recalls how he arranged for a friend to photograph the motif of a discarded Christmas tree that he found lying in a San Francisco street during the first week of January 1964. He sets the "psychological framework"[59] by noting "I think we were still in shock over President Kennedy's assassination" (42) and relates his reflections on the tree to the tragedy. The sight of the tree draws memories of a fallen soldier: "The tree had been stripped of its decorations and lay there sadly [...] A week before it had been a kind of hero" (43). A different tree sparks other associations: "the tree had the same candor as Saint Sebastian, arrows and all" (46), a reference to the early Christian martyr who is the patron saint of the dying. The initial nondescript image of a "dead soldier" becomes more sharply focused here into one who has fallen in the service of a good cause. The personification "assassinated Christmas" (43) establishes a direct link with the assassination, alluding to the somber mood of the nation in the run-up to the Christmas holiday after Kennedy's death: "terrible, illuminated by all the flags in America hanging at half-mast week after week in December like a tunnel of mourning" (42). In a conversation with the author, Brautigan confirmed that his intention here was to portray the feeling of "bleakness"[60] induced by the nation's still fresh sense of loss, an emptiness in the wake of dashed hope. Given the promise of a new beginning at the heart of both the joyful tidings of Christmas for Christians and Kennedy's inspirational New Frontier agenda for America, "assassinated Christmas" represents loss of faith in the future.

The question posed in the title "What are you going to do with 390 photographs of Christmas trees?" is raised once again within the text. The poet Lawrence Ferlinghetti observes the picture taking and asks in passing "Taking pictures of Christmas trees?" (46). The elusive reply "sort of", followed by the thought "*Does he know what we are doing?*" highlighted in italics, indicates that there is more going on here than meets the eye. This exchange pointedly reveals the author's view of the role of the artist in the situation at hand. For him, this role is to mitigate the steady advance of forgetting. With the many snapshots of the discarded Christmas trees the photographer is documenting – and simultaneously counteracting – "the journey away from Christmas" (43). With his text Brautigan aims to impact in an identical way the aborted new beginning for America consigned to oblivion by Kennedy's death.

“What are you going to do with 390 photographs of Christmas trees?” is followed by a further 72 texts which address other material before the narrator returns to the subject of the tragedy in the segment titled “A different way of looking at President Kennedy’s assassination.” The “different way” in this title offers a variation on the theme of the earlier text. This time, instead of the connection with Christmas, the President’s death is related to the relatively trivial circumstance of the narrator failing to be served the dish of his choice in a restaurant. The discordance between this banal incident and the killing of the President reflects the force of the assassination’s impact deep into the mundane regions of everyday life. When a commonplace moment of inconsequential irritation and disappointment calls to mind the loss engendered by the murder, it would thus seem that this loss has come to represent the epitome of disillusionment and senselessness: “Suddenly you think of President Kennedy. Your eyes fill up with tears” (145).

There is an absence of any recognizable continuity, causality or central plot line in the sequence of texts which appear between the Kennedy segments in the book. There is no obvious structure, so the reader is left confronted only with a disjointed series of disparate fragments. Although seemingly incoherent, the passages nevertheless form a narrative whole when taken together because the individual parts are bound together by an overarching theme and an underlying progression. What becomes exposed is a complex dynamic of permanency and transience layered with composition and decomposition. The Kennedy passages, which are the only texts that relate to one another, define two fixed demarcation points in this process, and in this way are featured with special prominence.

Brautigan provides the book with a unifying theme by counterbalancing vanitas motifs and their associations of transiency on the one hand with attempts to recall and retain on the other. For some of the texts this focus on death and transience is already apparent in their titles: “A death in Canada”, “Very good dead friends”, “The tomb of the unknown friend”, “Drowned Japanese boy”, “The man who shot Jessie James”, “Seventeen dead cats” and “A study in thyme and funeral parlors”, along with “A different way of looking at President Kennedy’s assassination”. The sketches of experiences and people are juxtaposed in a tension-laden manner, some of them serving to keep memory alive and shielded from dissolution, others emphasizing the loss of that which has passed away, such as in “What are you going to do with 390 photographs of Christmas trees?” They explore the varied ways and the extent to which memories can be retained, how they can be rescued from fading as time moves on, and ultimately preserved from disappearing completely. There is a wide variety of modes of preserving things and recording experience in *The Tokyo-Montana Express* ranging from old diary entries at the beginning of the book to more modern media communication at the end. Some of the ways do not actually work, for example when the narrator in “The smallest snowstorm on record" unsuccessfully tries to store snowflakes in the refrigerator. But retaining experiences by means of texts can also prove difficult, a problem exposed in the very first section of the book with diary entries of which only fragments are left. This renders them incapable of effectively fulfilling their intended purpose to document a span of time in a person's life. They themselves are subjected to transience and prove unable to preserve experience so as to prevent some period of a lifetime from being forgotten. The narrator fills in the resulting gaps with his own speculations. The jarring fragmentation contained in this initial text passage continues to reappear throughout the entire book.

Understanding the relationship between the individual fragments and the work as a whole is helped by the book's use of compositional images and also its publication history. Due to their titles, the way they appeared in print and, above all, their highly individual textual nature, Brautigan's narrative works often defy classification as short stories or book chapters. While some of his works can be identified as novels from their titles, such as *Dreaming of Babylon. A Private Eye Novel 1942* and *The Hawkline Monster. A Gothic Western*, other works give rise to puzzling dual interpretations. Sections from the full text of *Trout Fishing in America,* for example, originally appeared in a number of journals as stand-alone pieces.

Brautigan directly addresses the categories of "chapter" and "story" before abandoning them completely by including two "Lost Chapters of *Trout Fishing in America*" in *Revenge of the Lawn: Stories 1962-1970*, works with titles that contain both terms. In this way he incorporates the excerpted texts into the larger work while continuing to preserve their autonomy. He transcends writing conventions, and moves toward abolishing them in order to show that sections of texts can retain an independent standing while at the same time belonging to a larger whole. This concept equally applies to *The Tokyo-Montana Express.* The book starts off by referring to itself as one comprehensive narrative:

> Though the Tokyo-Montana Express moves at great speed, there are many stops along the way. This book is those brief stations: some confident, others still searching for their identities.
>
> The 'I' in this book is the voice of the stations along the tracks of the Tokyo-Montana Express. (7)

Yet sections of this book have also made separate appearances not only in *San Francisco Stories*, but also in such diverse periodicals as *Esquire, California Living, Earth, Triquarterly, Mademoiselle,* and *Evergreen*. Suzanne M. Sweatt therefore concludes: "While the diverse mini-chapters make this appear to be a short story anthology, the unifying themes and a dominant metaphor proclaim that this is indeed another Brautigan novel.[61] This take on the book, together with Claudia Großmann's description of *The Tokyo-Montana Express* as "a collection of short stories presented as a novel",[62] illustrate the difficulty of assigning this work to a standard literary genre. Brautigan breaks with convention to favor instead a way of writing that simultaneously combines autonomy and being part of something.

This simultaneity also exists within the text passages themselves, such as in "The menu/ 1965", one of the book's longest segments. The narrator is compiling observations, commentaries and other details about the death row tract at San Quentin Prison, including the dinner menu for a week in April 1965 which he has obtained by request. First he contemplates the menu himself, and then he shows it to friends for their reactions. The feedback that he gathers is textually integrated into the text which forms "The menu/ 1965". The food plan is not just a means of accomplishing the transition from a factual, real-life situation to its literary treatment. It also illustrates Brautigan's approach to depicting the relationship between a given whole and the various parts it is comprised of. He further heightens the resulting effect by inserting indented excerpts from the menu between text passages:

Beef Noodle Soup
Cole Slaw
Sour Cream Dressing
Grilled Halibut Steak
Cocktail Sauce
Chicken Fried Steak
Risotto
Btrd. Cauliflower (125)

By combining food into a menu whose specific dishes retain their individual character while at the same time forming part of a complete meal demonstrates how independent components can contribute to a larger whole without losing their identity. Furthermore, in the way that separate courses can be mixed together to make up an assortment of different meals, so too do texts combined in separate narratives retain their own identity in varying contexts.

Brautigan's self-referencing use of compositional food images and his placement of them throughout the text serve to illustrate how separate entities can both form part of and contribute to a larger whole. Given Kennedy's overall importance to the theme of the book, a further, more deeply embedded reference to the democratic principle of public participation emerges here expressed in his much quoted admonition "ask not what your country can do for you, ask what you can do for your country."[63]

In the way that Brautigan's fiction defies conventional classification, the author himself is difficult to assign to a given group or movement of thought. Stereotyping him as spokesman for the West Coast avantgarde falls somewhat wide of the mark, as does characterizing him as a cult figure of the Woodstock generation based on his popularity on college campuses, his role as a social critic, and his interest in issues such as ecology and social change. Other designations that endeavor to label him also fall short, including black humorist, genre parodist or a Beats and Hips go-between figure of the San Francisco Renaissance. This strong sense of independence and participation, of deconstruction and reconstruction, also marks his works and the democratic creed expressed in them, in particular with reference to Kennedy in *The Tokyo-Montana Express* – another specifically postmodern contribution to the collective memory of JFK.

Overcoming conventional schemes of classification is an inherent tenet of postmodernism. Exposing the inadequacy of traditional means of categorization and developing techniques to break these categories down into more elemental principles of conceptual understanding is a key characteristic of postmodern literature. According to DeLillo and McCaffery, the origins of this can be traced back to the loss of coherence and self-assuredness brought about by Kennedy's death. This is not to say that the notion of dissolution is limited to postmodern narratives with their inherent affinity for such phenomena. Instead, it is discernible that other contemporary literary references to disintegration also relate back in specific to the presidential murder. They surface in narratives which do not fall under the postmodern rubric, but which are nevertheless manifestly infused with the new awareness identified by DeLillo and McCaffery.

One example in this vein is John Updike's prominent use of allusions to dissolution in connection with the events of November 22, 1963 in his novel *Couples*. In this narrative general news of the Kennedys is first synchronized into the unfolding plot to provide contemporary coloring and chronological structure. The novel is set in the fictional town of Tarbox, based on Ipswich, Massachusetts where Updike lived for seven years. He portrays the promiscuous morals of ten prosperous, married couples whose professional, private and intimate paths cross, leading to the eventual breakup of several of the marriages. The events in Dallas occur midway in this process. The hedonistic group's ringleader, Fred Thorne, first hears of the shots fired at the President's motorcade on the radio in his dental office. His first reaction is to attribute the deed to "some crazy Texan",[64] but his assistant is quick to point a finger at communist agitators. Updated radio announcements shortly thereafter reveal the full extent of the tragedy: "The President had been shot at, the President had been hit, he had been hit in the head, his condition was critical, a priest had been summoned, the President was dead" (325).

The Thornes have difficulty making up their mind about cancelling the party they have planned for that evening, in particular since the liquor has already been purchased. After deciding to redub the affair "an Irish wake" (327), however, they reassure each other that they should go ahead with their plans and quickly manage to recoup their usual upbeat party mood. At the edge of the dance floor, with the party in full swing, Harold Little-Smith asserts that the assassin is probably a "*right*-wing crackpot" (330) given Dallas's notoriety as a bastion of political conservatism. To the relief of his fellow Republican friends he also declares that Oswald does not belong to their political party: "it wasn't one of ours, it was one of *theirs*!" (330) Fred Thorne voices his doubts about Oswald being the sole assassin: "He wasn't in it alone. There were too many shots. The whole fucking thing was too successful" (331). Little-Smith puts a Vietnamese hitman behind the murder as "punishment for his [Kennedy's] letting our one staunch ally in Southeast Asia get nailed to please the pansy left in this country" (351). Only the more sensitive Piet Hanema needs urging to join the dancing. He holds back, feeling that "it seems blasphemous, waltzing on the poor guy's grave" (338). He finally moves off as "it seemed that the couples were gliding on the polished top of Kennedy's casket" (344).

This scene seems tragicomic. Joyce Carol Oates writes: "What might be tragic can be reexamined, reassessed, and dramatized as finally comic."[65] The jarring effect of weaving humor into calamity serves to heighten the impact of the scene's implicit tragedy. It also exposes a collective decadence manifested not just on a small-town scale in the promiscuous Tarbox partner-swapping and marriage breakups, but also on a national scale in the paradigm of destruction and decline linked to the death of the President – "death and decay are subtly pervasive."[66]

In the novel the machinations of the married couples are called "a conspiracy to protect each other from death" (331). The author creates a 20th-century suburban version of *carpe diem* New England-style in the fresh wake of birth control and the sexual revolution with prose that is often sexually explicit. But the death of the President, in the way that it casts a shadow over the Thornes' party, likewise hangs like a dark cloud over them, serving as a constant reminder that death is inescapable and that the attempts to evade transience and the march of time will ultimately prove futile. From this point in the story onward the forces of dissolution gain momentum in a process which Tony Tanner has likened to entropy,[67] a development reinforced through repeated references to both structuredness and "shapelessness" (331), ranging from reflections on molecular configurations and architectural structures in the buildings erected by Piet Hanema's construction company to the web of personal relationships intertwining the members of the hedonistic Tarbox social circle. Everything degenerates: The couples go from "decay to disintegration" (124). In the second half of the novel, construction materials appear to be out of plumb and the revelation that one of the friends is suffering from cancer introduces an element of disorder that Piet views as "chaos of particles on the floor of matter" (473). Updike here describes a loss of order and stability ensuing from Kennedy's death comparable to his contemporaries who articulated this loss in a postmodern fashion.

Wright Morris's *One Day* contains some of the central elements of *Couples* transported to the west coast. His novel mirrors Updike's with its small-town setting and a plot intruded upon midway by news of the assassination. The day in the title refers to Friday, November 22, 1963 as it runs its course in Escondido, California, south of San Francisco.

Life along the blocks of the town's main square is a microcosm of ever repeating daily interactions. The leading citizens are the veterinarian Dr. Cowie and Sheriff McNamara, whose name triggers an immediate association with Kennedy by calling to mind Robert McNamara who served in his cabinet in a related public safety role as defense minister. Escondido's strong sense of community cohesion is shaken up by the return of Alec Cartwright, a student who spent time in Paris and participated in civil rights protests in the South, where she joined the Freedom Riders. She represents the social opposite of the complacent Cowie and the other characters similarly mired down in the trivialities of daily life. Alec aspires to social change. Now that she is back in town she attempts to provoke the locals out of their passivity and indifference with a shocking act by placing her newborn baby in the adoption basket of the animal shelter run by her mother. The anticipated backlash of outrage, however, is overshadowed by the news from Dallas.

The concept of time, how time rules over the day and its unfolding events and realizations, is omnipresent throughout the book. This is immediately evident from the time-of-day section headings used to structure the narrative, and the many references to clocks, parking meters and other kinds of time-measuring devices. There is the gong of the half-hourly news program marking the tempo of the passing hours, the routine activities happening as usual ("she would now sleep like dead until quarter past eight, at which time she would prepare the children for school: there were few eleven o'clock movies she ever switched off"),[68] and many references to specific times in the day: "too late he noticed the clock in the lobby: four minutes to eight. The ironclad rule was not to call her until ten o'clock" (43) or "what time was it? The blinker on the corner switched over to a stop light at nine thirty" (174).

Time, the story's structural reference for anchoring everything in its place, loses its stability and becomes transformed with Kennedy's death. As if mentioning time zones Morris writes that "it is Sunday morning in Dallas, but in Escondido it is still Friday" (334), dismissing the actual two hour time difference between the cities to infer instead that there are differences between "time of the sort one sees on a clock's face" (170) and the time one perceives. Some characters look at their watch and ask themselves "had it stopped?" (204, 325). There is talk of a "timeless void" (204) and life in "a timeless capsule" (403). This progresses to the point where all useful indicators of time malfunction, be it in the afternoon when "the clock on the bank reads 11:34" (321), or later with the question "who could say when this day had begun, or would ever end" (25). After the assassination occurs time is described as being "out of joint" (10), and the author makes the reader experience this disjointedness directly. The past tense used up to this point is simply discarded:

> Cowie palmed a clear spot on the glass and stared into the fog. Gone. Smoke the color of ashes canceled the square. Loud and clear a time signal sounded, but the voice of the announcer was hoarse and weak. He too would be glad when it was over. The cook, Tod Bemis, wheeled to raise his arm and turn up the volume. Sheriff McNamara, to spare the tired waitress the long walk around the counter, then heads for the door as if summoned to duty, leaving Cowie, the cook, and Mildred Popkin with the news of the hour. It is the same as it has been all day. Incomprehensible. They hear it without hearing. (25)

Parallel to gradually eliminating indications of time, the expanding force of degeneration has now begun to play on the characters' spatial orientation, awareness and understanding as well. Despite wiping the glass pane clean, Cowie cannot see the square while looking through the window due to the fog. The news bulletin is not only acoustically unintelligible, its meaning is also "incomprehensible"; the characters listen to the news but they do not understand what it is saying – "they hear it without hearing."

The fog is a leitmotif and key metaphor employed by Morris. It slowly thickens in the course of the novel to progressively impair all visual perception to the point of blocking it out completely. Just after the assassination the author describes the square as "fog-dimmed" (314). The fog then becomes, in turn, a "glowing veil" (324), a "thickening bank" and a "shroud" (23), until its full impact is finally attained: "The square and all it contains seems about to dissolve in the fog" (24). Morris explicitly emphasizes the altered perceptions that result: "the fog is dramatic in the way it transforms the familiar things into strange ones" (7); "the square stands empty as a country graveyard" (7); and "the fog seemed to shroud them" (332) along with "the shroud of fog" (23) which play upon the double meaning of "shroud" as both a protective wrap and a burial cloth. Here is a stark link of imagery connecting the theme of death and the presidential murder; in the second half of the book there is an ever advancing decline in order and perceptual capabilities. As to the force of the enveloping fog, Morris writes: "behind it lie the disordered events of the day" (21).

Similar to Eugene O'Neill's metaphoric use of fog in *Long Day's Journey into Night*, his drama depicting actions that likewise take place between the morning hours and midnight of a single day, the fog in *One Day* accompanies time as it progresses towards not just actual, but also symbolic darkness. Morris employs fog as a metaphor for hidden reality to illustrate how "incomprehensible" the actual reality of this particular day has become.

Joseph J. Eydeven describes *One Day* as Morris's "attempt to come to terms with the assassination of John F. Kennedy"[69] and as "a meditation on the meaning of Kennedy's assassination for American culture" (126). Morris, who said that "[it] paralyzed my imagination" (125), directly confronts his characters with the tragedy. In the moment of heightened awareness that follows, they experience what David Stevenson calls "[a] sudden need for meaning or coherence"[70] to compensate for the loss of these things. What they find instead is just the opposite: incomprehensibility and dissolution. Thus Morris, who uses Escondido and its local citizenry as stand-ins for American culture at large, arrives at much the same conclusions as DeLillo, Brautigan, and Updike and enhances them in the collective memory.

The same is also the case in William Manchester's *The Death of a President*. In their search just months after the assassination for someone to write an authorized version of the events that had transpired in Dallas, Jackie and Robert Kennedy turned to Manchester, who had already published *Portrait of a President: John F. Kennedy in Profile* to admiring reviews. Manchester's contract provided him with access to family members and associates for exclusive interviews and an advance of $36,000 to be paid by the publisher, while earmarking the book's supplemental royalties for the Kennedy Presidential Library. It also granted the family the right to approve the manuscript before publication. Kennedy's widow and brother subsequently objected to Manchester's giving the serialization rights to the manuscript to *Look* magazine for $665,000, and the controversy made headlines for weeks. The dispute was eventually resolved out of court and both the serialization and the book appeared in 1967. Controversy of a different nature also surrounded the book in connection with certain unflattering remarks it contained by Robert Kennedy about Lyndon B. Johnson and his behavior in the aftermath of the murder. The President's brother, who at the time was already contemplating running as a presidential candidate in the 1968 election, was branded in some quarters as ruthless for his attempts to have the potentially politically damaging passages eliminated before the book reached the market.[71]

In *The Death of a President* Manchester reconstructs the six days between the 20th and the 25th of November 1963, including the preparations for the trip to Texas, the events that ensued there and the funeral in Washington's Arlington National Cemetery. He devoted two years of research to the project which entailed interviews, eyewitness reports, photo, film and document analysis, visits to the various sites and a meticulous review of the timing of each occurrence related to the incident. He concludes that Oswald was the sole assassin.

Along with the authenticity that his investigation produced, however, literary elements also find their way into Manchester's account. These stem from his choice of an omniscient narrator, his interweaving approach to incorporating the many related events, and the mythopoetic overtones he includes in telling his version of what happened.

Rather than presenting his findings in a straightforward report, Manchester opts for an all-knowing narrator who is not just aware of the documented facts, but who also registers such intangibles as the mindset of key (historical) figures and, importantly, circumstantial details, background information and how things cohere. This element of fiction is used to several ends. For one, it helps lend a measure of added credence to the theory of Oswald as the lone gunman beyond the factual level. Secondly, employing such a point of view helps establish strong reader identification with Kennedy as the main character by tapping into a system of common values shared alike by the reader and the narrator. Thirdly, use of the omniscient narrator in combination with a non-linear structure helps to endow the incidents with deeper meaning than can be wrought by presenting the bare facts alone. Because his point of view is all-encompassing, the narrator can establish connections to actions that happen at different times, or at the same time but in different places. Manchester takes advantage of these options to structure *The Death of a President* as an assortment of erstwhile decisions and intersecting avenues of action seen in flashback rather than as a chronological summary of data and facts. The various narrative strands, separated into sequences, run at first parallel to one another chronologically, then pick up speed as they begin to converge and finally come together with the murder in Dallas, only to move off in different directions in the wake of the incident. As in *Libra*, the murder of the President serves as both the focal point of the plot and the story's compositional fulcrum.

To achieve this narrative structure, and also to incorporate earlier dated material into the November 20th to 25th timeframe, the author works with retrospections. As stepping stones to the past he avails himself of conversations, letters, places and even chance happenings. An example of this technique is the way he steers the plot line from the actions of White House naval assistant Oliver S. Hallet on the night of November 20th to details of Oswald's stay in Russia in 1959, and then back to 1963 and Oswald's deed in Dallas.

While Kennedy is hosting a reception at the White House the evening before departing for Texas, Hallet is working on finalizing the itinerary for the trip in the Situations Room. Hallet had previously served as a marine attaché in Moscow, where his wife worked as a receptionist at the American Embassy. She was the employee there that Oswald first approached in October 1959 about relinquishing his American citizenship. But Manchester does not just use the Hallets as a tie-in for a flashback and for transitioning from one plot strand and location to another. He also attributes the existence of such a coincidence to destiny. In describing the night of the 20th he mentions that "every frontier was as silent as fate"[72] and he refers to Hallet's White House connection as "uncanny destiny" (31). Donald Pizer identifies Manchester's implication here "that there is an inherent significance in the chronological relationship between events."[73]

The flashback is expanded when it gets to Oswald and Dallas to examine the security preparations of the FBI and the Dallas police department for the upcoming visit, including the written warning to the President's advisors that the city was not secure enough. Manchester reports how the security team inspected the route of the motorcade and found the School Book Depository on Elm Street a high risk, but then took no further follow-up action. They furthermore failed to conduct a routine investigation of Oswald, who was officially on record as a potential threat. The text highlights that these omissions were all the more surprising given the palpable anti-Kennedy sentiment among local Dallas rightwing groups which viewed the President's political agenda to be too soft and too liberal. This climate of heightened tension should have logically warranted special vigilance.

The approach the author selects for bringing all of these individual incidences together to form a coherent case might aim to stress causality or intentionality or, alternatively, might instead try to derive meaning from overlaps in timing and location. In the former, Oswald would come across as a tool or accomplice of the security agencies, or in other words as part of a conspiracy. In the latter, it would appear that the way was paved for the crime to happen by the haphazard shortcomings of the security apparatus. Because Manchester's documentary approach to telling the events restricts him to the verifiable facts, however, this second option is the only one available to him. Questions are duly raised as to whether the people assigned to protect the President were negligent in carrying out their responsibilities, and if the politically agitated mood in Dallas was a contributing factor to the murder. Ultimately, however, Manchester can only look to a chain of unrelated events that came together that day by pure chance for answers to questions about an explanation of the crime.

Manchester does not see the meaninglessness inherent at the core of this conclusion to be a product of the times and a part of a postmodern condition like DeLillo. He wants to suggest to the reader a way to deal with it. The strategy he adopts is to add an explanation of fate as a self-fulfilling prophesy for pursuing purpose and gleaning meaning alongside the tragic series of coincidences that form his Kennedy tale. This is evident throughout the main body of the work at those points where the confluences of time and place appear inevitable. But it is in his epilogue that Manchester expounds more explicitly on his view that destiny plays a role even in the most chance encounters. Under the heading "Legend" he mentions the mythological archetype of the "ritualistic murder of the folk hero" (623) as featured in works such as Mary Renault's historical novel *The King Must Die*.

Writing about the life of Theseus, the Greek mythological figure best known for slaying the monster Minotaur, Renault describes how his willingness to accept a preordained death is an insignium of his leadership:

> Horses go blindly to the sacrifice; but the gods give knowledge to man. When the king was dedicated, he knew his moira. In three years, or seven, or nine, or whenever the custom was, his term would end and the god would call him. And he went consenting, or else he was no king, and power would not fall on him to lead the people […] this was his sign: that he choose short life with glory, and to walk with the god, rather than live long, unknown like the stallfed ox.[74]

Moira refers to an individual's destiny and personal fortune; it is personified in Greek mythology as the three Fates or Moirai. Moira is attributed to the young Theseus, who later becomes a wise hero-king of Athens, as "the finished shape of our fate, the line drawn round it. It is the task the gods allot us, and the share of glory they allow […] and our appointed end."[75]

It proves impossible for Manchester to extract any sense of rational meaning from the theory of the assassination as the act of a lone and marginal character. He thus turns to the myth of the ancient king's self-sacrificial demise, and its suppositions that a predetermined death is one attribute of an exceptional leader. But Manchester fails to successfully achieve a contemporary adaptation of the myth for mid-twentieth century America. His inability to find adequate meaning transforms his mythopoetic expediency into a mythopoetic pitfall, and in effect hoists Kennedy to the status of myth with the predestined, extraordinary characteristics of a hero–ruler. In this manner, and despite aiming for factual authenticity, *The Death of a President* materially contributes to Kennedy's mythification.

Similar myth-making can be found in non-fiction about the assassination as well, a response that is perhaps rooted in a collective need to come to terms with history. Michael Beschloss, for example, alludes to the idea of self-sacrificial death in *Presidential Courage* when he writes of the murder paving the way for ground-breaking legislative reform:

> After John Kennedy's murder, his successor persuaded Congress to pass his civil rights proposals as the late President's most fitting memorial. Thus, by dying at the moment he did, Kennedy had ensured the success of the bill that would so change the nation.[76]

By combining factual documentation with literary and mythopoetic devices Manchester turns his work into a textual hybrid, and he himself terms *The Death of a President* a "narrative" (ix). Against the background of the New Journalism style of reporting, that also fuses fictional and non-fictional elements and was popularized in the 1960's and 1970's by the likes of Tom Wolfe, Truman Capote, and Norman Mailer, Donald Pizer narrows this description down further to "documentary narrative."[77] Seymour Krim calls the book an "imaginative and yet factual portrait"[78] and John C. Hartsock claims it is "impossible to place within traditional classification schemes."[79] With this shattering of conventional divisions separating genres to the point of abolishing them, the element of dissolution at the core of *Libra*, *The Tokyo-Montana Express*,

Couples, and *One Day* works its way at the compositional level into Manchester's book as well.

Beyond notions such as loss and bleakness the postmodern and traditional narratives each treat the disruptiveness of Kennedy's death in their own way. They both reflect and shape the collective memory. The authors share the aim of producing work that helps uncover some hidden truth, some sense, and collective understanding of the events in Dallas. DeLillo and Manchester approach this in exactly opposite ways. DeLillo goes about this by creating a work of fiction, but in so doing tries to stay as true as possible to the facts. Manchester, on the other hand, aims to write a historically accurate account of the murder as a work of non-fiction, but he turns for help in telling his account to the mythopoetic devices of fiction. Mastering the challenge to truth posed by the assassination thus proves to be unsolvable for both fiction and non-fiction. This conundrum perhaps shines a further revealing light on the openness and creativity required in attempting to come to terms with Kennedy's death.

Washington

> He'd call Rusk.
>
> No, he wouldn't call Rusk. Yes, he'd better call Rusk. No, dammit he wouldn't call Rusk.
>
> Yes, he'd better call Rusk, even if the State Department couldn't do anything right. But he'd better call Dillon.[80]

The President finds himself in a dilemma. After much indecisive deliberation and repeated hesitation he still cannot bring himself to contact the cabinet member in charge, Secretary of State Dean Rusk.

In *See You Later Alligator* William F. Buckley highlights two key themes related to John F. Kennedy right at the start of this novel: conflict and breaking new ground. By zooming in on Kennedy, and simultaneously showing not only his observable actions but also his train of thought, Buckley contributes to a character sketch in this episode. It takes place in the first year of Kennedy's presidency and presents him facing the most dangerous political confrontation in history.

Although acute crises are common in politics, they came to be a defining mark of the Kennedy Administration for occurring so frequently and with such exceptional magnitude. As early as Inauguration Day 1961 James Reston commented in the *New York Times* that "the problems before the Kennedy Administration are much more difficult than the nation has yet come to believe."[81] The new government's daily agenda was crowded with such a barrage of domestic and foreign policy matters that in his first year in office Kennedy publicly admitted:

> When I ran for the presidency of the United States, I knew that this country faced serious challenges, but I could not realize – nor could any man realize who does not bear the burdens of this office – how heavy and constant would be those burdens.[82]

On the domestic front, it was becoming increasingly urgent to resolve the civil rights issue. The problems abroad stretched from Laos and Vietnam in Asia, across the Middle East, Congo and Berlin, over to Latin America where Cuba was causing significant concern. Although different with respect to origin, regional intensity and global impact, all of these trouble spots were linked to the Cold War, which escalated dramatically in October 1962 with the Cuban Missile Crisis. This confrontation came to be the Cold War's climax, as well as its turning point. It generated experiences and insights that set the major world powers on the path towards reducing aggressive military engagement and induced them to seek alternatives to direct confrontation for maintaining their coexistence.

The way people react to a crisis situation can often serve to reveal fundamental facets of their character. In the case of John Kennedy, the crisis in autumn 1962 is particularly well suited for this purpose because, distinct from the other major national and international conflicts he faced, its beginnings did not predate his administration. Unlike the Vietnam War or the civil rights question, issues which extended well beyond the span of his term in office, the Cuban Missile Crisis offers up an isolated instance of unfolding events and decision-making for observing Kennedy in power up close.

The structure of Buckley's novel bears exceptional affinity with its historical setting. The association is strong both thematically and structurally because it centers, like the time period in history, on a bipolar split. The opposing geopolitical divide of East versus West establishes the underlying dichotomy of the Cold War. In a spy novel the dichotomy is created with two camps serving as opposing fronts between which operative agents maneuver. At the very minimum these fronts coexist competitively, but more often than not they interact confrontationally. Further dichotomies are frequently added, a clash of friend versus foe for example. Fact and fiction constitute another opposed pair. The distinction between fact and fiction is never fully discernable, however, in part because politicians and intelligence agencies (must) withhold information. As a result, relevant facts are only revealed in bits and pieces and are never fully verifiable in the text.

What William F. Buckley created with *See You Later Alligator* is a literary adaptation of the Cuban missile incident in the form of a spy novel. The core of his story contains two chains of authentic events about which the general public had only limited knowledge at the time. The first is connected to Kennedy's decision-making dilemma at the very start of the book. An opportunity arises on the one hand to take a tentative first step toward reaching an understanding with Cuba. On the other hand, however, such a move carries incalculable political risk given the rapid deterioration and growing ideologization in the strained relations between the two countries just several months after the failed Bay of Pigs coup attempt.

The President, only in office since the start of the year, had inherited plans for a Cuban commando raid from the outgoing Eisenhower Administration. Cubans in exile were trained in Guatemala with the help of the CIA for an invasion aimed at sparking the initial flames of a populist revolution against the regime of Fidel Castro. The operation ended in the infamous military and political fiasco in Kennedy's fourth month in office, turning Cuba into one of his biggest headaches.

When an opportunity to reestablish direct dialogue with Cuba surfaces several months later, in August 1961, not only Secretary of State Dean Rusk but also most of Kennedy's other political, military and intelligence advisors are kept in the dark. For them, as well as for the American public at large, the effort to restore relations can only be reconstructed later. It emerges from talks conducted that month by a U.S. delegation under Treasury Secretary Douglas Dillon with Latin American economic ministers in the town of Punta del Este, a beach resort near Montevideo, Uruguay. The conference is organized through an initiative of the Kennedy Administration aimed at offering the countries of Latin America a program of economic and democratic development called "The Alliance for Progress". An explosive backlash ensues, caused not by the negotiated package of cooperation reforms, but by a clandestine meeting which occurs outside of the official program. A Kennedy aide meets secretly with Cuban representative Che Guevara, the first high-ranking contact between the two countries.

Richard Goodwin, a close advisor to the President on Latin American matters, speaks with Guevara in Uruguay about a potential *modus vivendi*, an agreement to disagree without the need to reach a compromise on every outstanding issue. Goodwin is not affiliated with the State Department, but he has an office in the White House and reports directly to the President. Leaks fueled by mistrust, particularly from the Republican opposition, create a political storm over the contact with Guevara and lead two weeks later to a Senate subcommittee investigation into the Cuban advances.[83] In a memo to Kennedy in mid-August Goodwin assesses the potential for easing tensions in an optimistic light and counsels for continuation of the "below ground dialogue."[84] As he recalls in his memoirs, though, he personally had no further contact with Che.[85] The historical record indicates that secret attempts to reach deténte in fact subsequently resumed by 1963 at the latest.[86] For the interval between those efforts and the meeting in Punta del Este, however, there is no evidence that any further "below ground" discussions took place. Thus there are only two possible conclusions: either these talks failed to occur, or they were fully successful in being held in complete secrecy. It is this specific historical loophole that Buckley seizes for his literary interpolation.

See You Later Alligator picks up the thread of the back channel operation as the President decides in favor of continued negotiations. From Uruguay the stage is set for talks to resume in Cuba three months later, in October 1961, under the mission code name *Projecto Caiman*. These efforts advance only feebly, however, and the eagerly anticipated announcement of a breakthrough is constantly postponed to subsequent meetings. For the American emissary, the novel's main character, Blackford Oakes, the situation is aptly summed up by Guevara's stereotypical farewell "Hasta luego, Caiman" – "See you later, Alligator" – at the end of each negotiating session. Oakes' stay in Cuba is extended month after month, interrupted only occasionally by short trips to Washington to report feedback. Eventually, relations between the two countries deteriorate to such an extent that Oakes is finally ordered home and his official status is terminated. But at his own request, and with Kennedy's approval, he returns to the island as Guevara's guest and continues to investigate further until his role in the book veers off on a different tangent.

This plot line closely follows the development of the actual crisis which began to fester in 1960, then escalated in mid-1962, and finally moved to the brink of nuclear war that same year in the thirteen days between October 16 and 28. At the root of the matter was a conflict over taking decisive action. A rapidly growing military build-up had been established on Cuba by that time with Soviet help. The Kennedy Administration faced heightened pressure to react when a succession of Russian ships landed on the island in July 1962 carrying weapons, technical experts and soldiers. This was followed in September by the discovery of Soviet fighter bombers with a range capable of reaching Florida and, shortly thereafter, entire missile bases. The administration had been able to cast the escalation developments as chiefly defensive activities for its critics on the home front until then. But maintaining this posture was proving to be increasingly problematic. A worried public called for resolute action. The U.S. military and members of the opposition led by Senators Goldwater and Keating publically urged the President to make a decisive move. Keating called Kennedy "our do-nothing President"[87] on national television. Clare Boothe Luce warned in *Life Magazine* that "what is now at stake in the decision of intervention or non-intervention in Cuba is the question not only of American prestige but of American survival."[88] On September 3 the *New York Times* wrote, "the administration is under Congressional pressure to intervene militarily in Cuba" and "Mr. Kennedy is caught between Cuban charges that he is planning to invade the island and mounting Congressional demands that he should do precisely this."[89] The Soviet Union, meanwhile, threatened that any military action against Cuba would start a war.

This foreign policy dilemma was further exacerbated by events playing out domestically. Incidents of racial conflict had worsened to the point that the President had federalized the National Guard and sent troops to the south to protect the lives of African American students at the University of Alabama. With upcoming fall congressional elections deepening the existing political divide, the government anticipated heated criticism if the general public perceived their response to blacks and communists as being too weak.

Until mid-October that year the full extent of the Soviet activities on Cuba remained hidden from America's military leaders due to poor aerial visibility conditions. But on October 15 U-2 reconnaissance planes finally managed to locate weapon depots, housing bases, trenches and, for the first time, evidence of medium range ballistic missiles with nuclear warheads capable of reaching targets on the American mainland. In the face of this intelligence, the administration in Washington feared it would pay a high price if no action were taken before time ran out. From a geopolitical perspective, the confirmed existence of such nuclear missiles would shift the prevailing East-West balance of power which up until then had evenly juxtaposed equivalent levels of military fear. The consequences for global security were incalculable, particularly for exposed flashpoints such as West Berlin. Equally worrisome was the loss of face America would suffer on the international stage. An election defeat would be guaranteed at home, transferring power to the Republican opposition which favored a military solution. Even at the very apex of the crisis, though, Kennedy refused to yield to the pressure to launch an airstrike to destroy the offensive weapons, as tape recordings with his advisors show. For him and his brother, this option strongly reeked of a surprise attack similar to another Pearl Harbor. It also carried potentially destructive consequences for West Berlin and heightened the likelihood of a nuclear confrontation with the Soviets.[90]

A crisis team, the Executive Committee of the National Security Council (ExComm), had assembled at the White House requiring a reliable assessment of the situation. Publicly, the Soviets were denying such a state of affairs on Cuba, but this contradicted covertly gathered intelligence from Moscow. Washington urgently needed to verify the U-2 reconnaissance photos. If the findings did prove to be valid, the President and ExComm needed to know how advanced the installations were. In short, the key questions were how ready were the sites for combat and how much time remained for crisis management, possible negotiation or eventual attack.[91] Any information gathered by intelligence agents at the site would clearly be of crucial importance.

Buckley takes up this spy assignment[92] and gives it to Blackford Oakes, retracing in *See You Later Alligator* the progress of his investigations on the island. In the intervals between his meetings with Guevara, Oakes begins to detect an increasingly hectic level of general activity and a sense of heightened secretiveness. He checks out the growing volume of vehicular traffic and eventually, with the help of his Cuban translator, discovers missiles nearly ready for deployment, along with Soviet and Cuban staff working to prepare them for engagement. When his cover is exposed at this point, Oakes smuggles the information out of Cuba in a suspenseful escape and delivers it to Washington in a race against time. By combining Oakes' intelligence with the analyses of the aerial surveys it becomes possible for Washington to positively identify the military presence on Cuba as offensive weapons and to estimate the stage of their combat readiness. This enables the President and ExComm to weigh all potential options for action and adroitly manage the situation through the use of timing tactics.

Kennedy and Oakes in effect become co-protagonists in surmounting this crisis on the cusp of a nuclear confrontation. The narrative focus on Kennedy, introduced with his mental deliberations in the initial lines of the novel, becomes forcefully intensified as the novel progresses through the author's choice of perspective and the way he combines factual and fictional details.

Buckley achieves a strong sense of verisimilitude in the novel in referring to many details typical for the time period by describing situations, places, settings and historical events, as well as personalities and their mannerisms, behaviors and ways of thinking. These details effectively serve to impart a heightened semblance of historical authenticity to his Kennedy character. Buckley's fictionalization of the initial meeting between Che Guevara and Richard Goodwin is a good example of just how closely his rendering of the incident follows the historical record. Goodwin writes in his memoirs:

> Guevara began by saying he wished to thank us for the Bay of Pigs. I said he was welcome. Their hold on the country had been a bit shaky, he explained, but the invasion allowed the leadership to consolidate most of the major elements of the country behind Fidel. Perhaps, I answered, they would return the favor and attack Guantanamo.[93]

This incident from Kennedy's perspective in *See You Later Alligator* becomes:

> *That was a nice wisecrack Guevara opened with: "I want to thank you for invading our country. It has made a great power out of us and eliminated all resistance to Castro." Well we had it coming. I like Dick's answer too: "You are welcome. And you can repay the favor by invading Guantanamo."* (3)

The novel's twin pairing of Kennedy and Oakes establishes two parallel lines which develop separate plotstrands, perspectives and compositional styles: one is a political tale, the other a spy story. The first provides the stage for the fictionalization of an historical figure, the second for a fictitious character. They are kept apart from one another in a deliberate way – Kennedy and Oakes never appear in the same scene and their crossdealings are portrayed only indirectly. Most strikingly, the two narrative strands are told from different points of view.

Oakes' activities are related from the outward-looking perspective of an authorial narrator in the third person. In Kennedy's case, the narration is often reduced to the point where unspoken words, feelings and mental associations are conveyed in a discernibly direct way to the reader through his thought process. The very first line of the book ("He'd call Rusk.") is one such example. The author achieves this effect through his frequent use of the literary devices of the narrated monologue and interior monologue, as in the following excerpt about one Goodwin-Guevara meeting:

> *I wonder. Dick did stress the secrecy. Fat chance his meeting will be secret for very long.* "Castro's No. 2 Man Meets / With Presidential Special Assistant. Che Guevara, Cuban Economic Czar, Spends Late Evening / With Richard Goodwin, JFK Speechwriter. They Met Privately in Montevideo / Reportedly Got On 'Famously.'" *Let's see, did I miss anything?Yeah.* "House Committee on Un-American Activities / Issues Subpoena of Goodwin / Aide pleads Executive Immunity." (2)

Another such example deals with the discovery of the missile bases on Cuba:

> *Not a sign of any missiles or missile sites in the U-2 photos taken on – I can memorize the dates. I've heard them so often – August 29, September 5, 17, 24, 28, 29, October 5. So I said, why not any flights since October 5? And McNamara says there was a flight scheduled for October 9, but the weather was bad. So I said how come we didn't fly on the 10th, and he said that was bad, too, bad right up until Sunday. Huh. That's when I pinned McCone down and finally got the story.* (2-3)

Snapshots from a fly-on-the-wall perspective[94] set the scene for such thought sequences:

> He rose from his desk and walked over to the rocking chair. Scooping up the afternoon's *Washington Star* from the coffee table. But although he spread the paper out on his lap, he didn't read it. He continued to think … (74)

Kennedy's mental monologues are distinctly set apart from the Oakes passages by appearing in the text in italics. The Kennedy and Oakes sections consistently constitute separate chapters as well, further reinforcing the dual-track structure. The Oakes segments follow the narrative model used by Ian Fleming for his James Bond novels: "assignment, contact, capture, escape and victory"[95]. The Kennedy chapters clearly stand out in superordinate fashion. Using historical facts and a maximum degree of historical accuracy to establish this strict separation also serves to heighten the impression of Kennedy's greater authority and his wealth of accumulated experience in contrast to Oakes.

Numerous biographical references correspond to the popular JFK image. These include mention of his school years at Choate, his time as a Harvard student, other Kennedy family members, details of his private life such as his prized rocking chair, and personality traits such as his admiration for quickwittedness, courage and style. Buckley does not draft these historical sketches and perceptions of Kennedy merely to have them remembered, but rather to reveal certain of his human qualities. Right from the start he exposes personality traits that underlie the popularly accepted image of Kennedy, focusing attention on the reasoning behind his decision-making and his negotiating conflicts. Kennedy speculates about the political mistake of the Bay of Pigs Invasion: "*that dumb thing we did in April, trying to take Cuba away from Castro. A half-assed operation, and I was responsible, I don't deny it*" (76); he reacts to presidential duties with dread: "*I'd like to change the timetable for Haile Selassie's visit to maybe 1981*" (75); he thinks about sex while waiting for his phone call to be put through to the Director of the CIA (3) and he must suppress his impatience during dinner speeches: "*some people don't know what a toast is* […] *Of course, be reasonable. The whole thing was being translated, which doubled its length. The* longeur *of the thing, as Jackie would put it*" (217); the interminable orations of Castro and Khrushchev astonish him:

> *Khrushchev speaking six and one half hours! I don't think I've ever heard anyone speak for one and one half hours, not even Hubert. Nice joke at the Al Smith dinner a couple of years*

ago: "What comes after a speech of Senator Humphrey on Saturday? Sunday." Well, maybe Hubert. But six and a half hours! What does the audience do for six and a half hours? What if they have to pee? (76)

He calls Latin American politicians who amass personal fortunes while in office "those buggers, the way they salt it away" (1); the double-dealing Soviet Foreign Minister is "a creep", (293) and Senator Keating is "full of baloney" (207).

Common, everyday uncertainties are blended into the scenes of political peril. In deliberating about the covert nature of Goodwin's mission to Montevideo, for example, Kennedy raises mundane questions about the time difference between Washington and South America:

Dick said the journalist in on the rendezvous promised he'd keep quiet, and – not so bad – the news isn't out yet, and I figure the meeting ended – let me see – oh – it's...11 p.m. When was it 6 a.m. in Montevideo, when their meeting broke up? I suppose I could call the Library of Congress and ask. Probably would take them two days to come up with the answer. Call it sixteen hours ago. I think Buenos Aires and Washington are on the same time zone. So nobody has come out with it yet. But they will, they will. (2)

A similar example portrays him contemplating a Soviet bomb test:

And so now Khrushchev is going to detonate a 50-megaton bomb. Five million tons. Or is that 50 million tons? Let me see: mega means a thousand, right? So fifty times a thousand is fiftythousand, that can't be right. Mega must mean a million. Then fifty megatons would be fifty million. Right? Right. (75-6)

Kennedy does not come across as a highly polished politician, nor is his character enhanced in any superlative way. Rather, the attributes of a competent statesman are accorded him along with his human qualities. The non-idealized depiction of Kennedy which results works to prevent the reader from disassociating from an aloof image. Buckley humanizes his Kennedy character, thereby effectively reducing the reader's distance to him. This in turn further augments the approachability Buckley achieves through his choice of narrative perspective. While historiographical or political accounts often draw out some generalization, in this literary text history and politics are related in a personalized way through the specific experiences of a given individual.

Kennedy 'the politician' appears in the novel as the person who is always one step ahead of the government bureaucracy in solving problems. He is the dependable crisis manager, someone capable of breaking down conflict-laden barriers of ideology. At the start of his term in office, before the problems with Cuba advance to the critical stage of the Missile Crisis, he focuses on assuaging the situation. As one of his priorities he strives to strike a new tone in the dialogue between the two countries. The extent to which this strategy sets its sights on a completely new course is reflected in the accompanying high political risks and unknowns. For this reason the President chooses to adopt a deinstitutionalized approach. He aims to break the deadlock of East-West confrontation in an innovative way by loosening the ideological moorings of the dichotomous world order. He calls into question the scheme of thinking and acting based on the hegemony of polarized value systems, along with all related classifications and boundaries. He presents himself as a statesman who, despite the risks, is unaligned with this predominant pattern of thought and who, instead, stands for reform, resolution and détente.

The strict East-West dichotomy is already undermined to an extent at the point when Kennedy and Guevara, as representatives of each respective power block, take their first steps to move closer together and jointly endeavor to pursue constructive cooperation instead of confrontational opposition. With the pairing of Kennedy and Guevara two charismatic personalities from this era in history are brought together in an early attempt to reach a mutual understanding. On a symbolic and emotional level both men by this time have become political icons. Against this backdrop each of them acquires individuality as a character in the novel, with the focus on Kennedy placing him clearly in the foreground.

In decision-making situations such as in the opening scene of the novel, the American President is portrayed as being wrenched in opposite directions. The narrative tempo is slow and synchronized with Kennedy's thought process so that the time it takes to read these passages matches the time of his first-hand mental train of thought. This technique helps to generate immediate empathy with what is taking place psychologically. This contrasts with the Oakes' sections of the book where, due to time lapses and gaps in the plot of the novel, the period covered in the narration is longer than the narrating time itself. Here there is the clear impression of experiences being recounted after the fact.

By placing the reader inside of Kennedy's thought process, characterizing his human qualities and adopting a vantage point from his perspective, the author orients the reader much closer to Kennedy than to Guevara and, by extension, toward the position of the West that he represents in the context of the Cold War. This reflects the novel's clear and consistent ideological stance. Buckley details, for instance, how Oakes' assistant, Cecilio Velasco, Trotsky assassin and former KGB major, experiences the dark side of the Soviet system and defects. He makes references to Stalinism and the subjugation of the East Block states, the Cuban government's delay tactics of negotiating in bad-faith and the secret installation of the offensive missiles. Buckley explains in his autobiography that in the Oakes novels, unlike the treatment of the CIA by Graham Greene or the MI-6 by John LeCarré and Len Deighton, he tried to differentiate the methods of the American secret service from those of the KGB.[96] He writes:

> To say that the CIA and the KGB engage in similar practices is the equivalent of saying that the man who pushes an old lady into the path of a hurtling bus is not to be distinguished from

> the man who pushes an old lady out of the path of a hurtling bus: on the grounds that, after all, in both cases someone is pushing old ladies around.[97]

According to Buckley, his motivation at the start of the Blackford Oakes series was to commit "literary iconoclasm"[98]: "I would write a book in which the good guys and the bad guys were actually distinguishable from one another. I took a deep breath and further resolved that the good guys would be – the Americans."[99] In this respect his books align with the basic ideological understanding found in Ian Fleming's adventures of James Bond. In *See You Later Alligator* Buckley underpins the East versus West confrontation with the type of good versus evil contrast often found in romances and fairy tales. Kennedy leads the charge of the good, and in so doing creates a certain sense of myth at a subliminal level. The more evil his adversaries from the opposite camp who encounter his peacemaking efforts, the more heroic he himself appears.

William F. Buckley, a noted conservative political journalist, the founder and publisher of the *National Review* and for over 30 years, from 1966 to 1999, host of the television talk show *The Firing Line* constructs his spy novel along the good versus evil axis that characterized the East versus West conflict, clearly making it a proponent of the West. What results is an ideological commentary encased in the dichotomical mind set of the Cold War. As a consequence, the novel in its entirety remains locked into exactly those modes of thought which its Kennedy character attempts to vanquish.

Norman Mailer, Buckley's political antithesis,[100] follows a similar formula for his novel *Harlot's Ghost*. His book is written in the same genre and deals with the CIA from the time of the Berlin Airlift until Kennedy's assassination. With the bipolar backdrop of the two opposing major world power blocs, this novel also focuses to a great extent on the Cuban Missile Crisis. Mailer's narrative is primarily told by CIA agent Herrik (Harry) Hubbard, who thinks back on his past and the nearly thirty years he has spent with the agency. His mentor is Hugh Tremont Montague, codenamed "Harlot", whose body is found washed up on a Chesapeake Bay beach with the face rendered unidentifiable by a gunshot wound. Montague was known to have been a leading counterspy, raising suspicions that he might have actually been a double agent who staged his own death in order to defect to the Soviet Union. In the hope of finding Harlot, Harry travels first to New York and then to Moscow where, sifting through documents in the Hotel Metropol, he is brought to reflect back on his CIA career.

Mailer abruptly intersperses narrative passages with other types of text excerpts such as authentic newspaper clippings, fictitious tape transcripts and letters, in particular those exchanged by the narrator and Hadley Kittredge, Harlots exwife, whom Harry marries. The novel's exceptionally loose form led John Simon to denounce the book's lack of structural coherence when it first appeared. He wrote:

Mailer here espouses just about all known and several unknown forms of fiction: *Bildungsroman*, epistolary novel, diary novel, phonecall novel, gossip-column novel, philosophico-political novel, pornographic novel and adventure story rotate into our field of vision.[101]

What Simon overlooked is that by presenting the narrative whole without any trappings of conventional transparency Mailer effectively emphasizes the novel's principal themes of ambiguity and insecurity. These aspects are not just expressed through the secretive dealings of the intelligence agents, the questionable identities, the confusing personal relationships and many permutations of deceitfulness – "uncertainty [is] the operative mode".[102] They are equally conveyed through the story's ill-defined and confounding form, and in this way passed along to the reader as part of the reading experience.

Mailer's technique of combining fictional and authentic texts is less a manifestation of the postmodern aesthetic than a reflection of his own demands on verisimilitude. He already treated the dividing line between fact and fiction in a nebulous way in earlier writings. *History as a Novel – The Novel as History*[103] the subtitle he gave to his book *The Armies of the Night*, is a typical example. Here, through use of the novel as metaphor, he diminishes historians' claim to objectivity in a manner reminiscent of his postmodern contemporaries John Barth, Thomas Pynchon and Don DeLillo:

So the Novelist working in secret collaboration with the Historian has perhaps tried to build with his novel a tower fully equipped with telescopes to study – at the greatest advantage – our own horizon. Of course, the tower is crooked, and the telescopes warped, but the instruments of all science – history so much as physics – are always constructed in small or large error.[104]

The way he understands fiction as a concept goes even further in *Harlot's Ghost,* where in the "Author's Afterword" he claims a literary account of the past to be more "real" than a non-fictional version:

It is the authors contention that good fiction [...] is more real, that is more nourishing to our sense of reality, than non-fiction, and so I mixed the factual with he fictional in order to prove a point: If the reader's imagination is rewarded with a large and detailed mural of a social organism moving through some historical events, then the reader's last concern is to be provided every instant with a scorecard of what actually happened and what was made up. My hope is that the imaginary world of *Harlot's Ghost* will bear more relation to the reality of these historical events than the spectrum of facts and often calculated misinformation that still surrounds them.[105]

Mailer argues that the novel can create "superior histories out of an enhancement of the real, the unverified, and the wholly fictional" (1133) and he underscores the close approximation to reality in *Harlot's Ghost* by stressing that "the events described are either real, or able to respect the proportions of the factual events" (1134). He in effect sketches a panorama where fictional and non-fictional passages stand side by side and fictitious characters interact with fictionalized historical personalities. Wilfried Sheed comments that "within the limits of celebrity mimicry, Mailer acquits himself ingeniously,"[106] a remark that appears to aptly apply with respect to some of his depictions of the latter.

For his Kennedy character, the demands that Mailer makes on verisimilitude are exceptionally high. Kennedy maneuvers at transition points in the narrative where the text types change and he appears in the varying fictionalized passages. But of all the book's characters, he alone is also presented in a series of authentic interviews which were conducted by the French journalist Jean Daniel. These were published in *The New Republic* on December 7 and 14, 1963 and subsequently integrated into the novel by Mailer. These actual statements are the only passages in *Harlot's Ghost* where Kennedy speaks in person; the rest of the time he is heard in Reported Speech. Furthermore, his actions are largely limited to the historical record. This awards him a high degree of credibility, which serves to differentiate him from the other historical characters.

The author's interest in Kennedy as a subject had already come to light in such previous works as an early article titled "Superman Comes to the Supermarket" about Kennedy's nomination as the Democratic presidential candidate in 1960 in Los Angeles; his novel *An American Dream* where in the very first sentence his protagonist tells of an encounter with his alter-ego "Jack Kennedy";[107] notably in *The Presidential Papers*, a collection of texts dedicated to John F. Kennedy in which Mailer sees himself as a "court wit" and "amateur adviser";[108] and finally in *Oswald's Story: An American Mystery*, a psycho-biography of the alleged assassin of Dallas which Mailer compiled as a contribution to shedding light on that tragic incident.

The Kennedy figure in *Harlot's Ghost* plays a centrally significant role. To this end, the author avails himself of popularly accepted Kennedy attributes, such as those which appear in the following authentic report by the journalist Daniel:

> President Kennedy received me at the White House on Thursday, October 24...As we passed through the small room where his secretary was working, we caught a glimpse of Mrs. Kennedy leaving by a French window on her way to a private garden of the White House. The President called her back to introduce me.
>
> It was still Indian summer in Washington. The weather was very warm and both the President and Mrs. Kennedy were very lightly dressed, thus enhancing the impression of youth, charm, and simplicity which was in rather surprising contrast to the solemnity of entering these august chambers. (1071)

His amorous affairs are accorded broad treatment as well. The perspective is particularly relevant here given the antagonism that existed between the President and Washington's security apparatus. This relates back to Kennedy's oppositional stance to the demands of his military and government advisors during the Bay of Pigs Invasion and the Missile Crisis, and his ultimate decision against taking military action. Harry's father, Cal Hubbard, a prominent CIA agent of the older generation, reproaches his son saying "I will only remind you that Kennedy dealt the CIA a blow at the Bay of Pigs from which we may never recover. We were slathered with shame. No, I will never forgive Jack Kennedy" (1093). Harry must concede "how much animosity is loose in the Agency these days toward our President" (1092). When Russian ships are heading straight for the defense line of the U.S. naval fleet positioned off the coast of Cuba during the blockade, one CIA agent formulates his support for military escalation by saying: "if we don't have a shooting war, Khrushchev will piss all over Kennedy in the negotiations" (988). The view of the secret service here is blatantly negative, so that it loses some of its bite when finding fault with Kennedy's philandering, such as when Cal Hubbard complains: "Jack reached the presidency with a long tail of big and little loves strewn behind him as the tin cans tied to a newly-wed's flivver. Yet never a hint in the major newspapers. A man running for high office is sacrosanct: twice so, once he is President" (1093). Heather Nielsen comments on Mailer's depiction of Kennedy as a "promiscuous and intensely ambitious yet morally responsible man, with a sharp and inquisitive intelligence."[109] She feels Kennedy's womanizing is treated too leniently and suspects this is because "Mailer valorizes Kennedy's heterosexual promiscuity as a sign of virility."[110] The President's behavior also has security implications as one of his lovers in the novel, Modene Murphy, is concurrently involved in a relationship with the Mafia boss Sam Giancana. In addition, Mailer mentions rumors of an affair with Marylin Monroe and the unresolved circumstances surrounding her death (1092-1094).

At the political level it is Kennedy's positive character traits that stand out. His resolute and consistent political posturing provides a counterpoint to the motifs of uncertainty and ambiguity found throughout the novel. "He didn't flap" (795) describes his firm stance with the Director of the CIA during the Bay of Pigs disaster and Kittridge stresses his "unflappability" (1017) during the days of crisis in October. Moreover, Kennedy serves as the counterbalance to the secret service, which as a destabilizing power proves itself to be a threat to democracy; this reinforces his positive role. Above all, however, he repeatedly resists the calls for implementing a military solution. Instead, he imposes a restraint of power which, in the end, contributes significantly to resolving the confrontation at the brink of atomic war in a peaceful manner. In this way he proves himself to be a politician with the perseverance and capabilities of carrying out the responsibilities of his office. The crisis likewise reveals Kennedy's strengths to the political observer Kittredge, who writes to Harry in a letter:

> What does remain alive for me is Jack's unflappability as the Russian freighters approached the line of quarantine. There are moments when great political leaders not only receive emoluments the of the gods, but their terrors. Is this too grandiose? I don't care. I love Jack Kennedy for finding is balance between two horrors, submission or extermination, and maintaining that balance through all the stunts that Khrushchev pulled after the Russian freighters turned around. I will tell you, Harry, that I did not really believe in Jack's pristine worth as a President before this happened. I liked him enormously because he had not gone dead inside like most major politicians [...]. Ditto Bobby. How could two Americans, well brought up, innocent as the well-to-do always are, manage not to panic? What bravery they showed at the core – to stay so long at the edge of the precipice! (1017-8)

Furthermore the openness of Kennedy's ideological stance pointed up by Buckley in *See You later Alligator* is forcefully underscored by Mailer in an interview with Daniel in which Kennedy comments on the American-dependent Batista regime toppled by Castro:

> To some extent it is as though Batista was the incarnation of a number of sins on the part of the United States. Now we have to pay for those sins. In the matter of the Batista regime, I am in agreement with the first Cuban revolutionaries.That is perfectly clear. (1071)

In contrast to Buckley, Mailer goes so far as to fracture the dichotomous framework of his narrative for his Kennedy character. His collage-like approach of stringing together different types of texts permits him to sever the dominant Western stance at certain points in the novel and insert the opposing view. Towards the end of the book he incorporates original passages from Daniel's interviews which reflect the standpoint of the Eastern power block from Castro's perspective. The Cuban leader comments on Kennedy, explaining that he considers him to be an honest politician (1085), and adds "I feel that he inherited a difficult situation" (1085). He welcomes Kennedy's Alliance for Progress reform initiative: "'... in a way' Castro said, 'it was a good idea, it marked progress of a sort, an effort to adapt to the extraordinarily rapid course of events in Latin America'" (1086). The Cuban head of state fears, however, that the President's positive new strategic approach will be, if nothing else, sabotaged from within:

> Suddenly a President arrives on the scene who tries to give the various Latin America countries the impression that the United States no longer stands behind the dictators. What happens then? The trusts see that their interests are being a little compromised; the Pentagon thinks the strategic bases are in danger; the powerful oligarchies in all the Latin American countries alert their American friends; they sabotage the new policy; and, in short, Kennedy has everyone against him. (1086-7)

At the same time he points out Kennedy's potential to solve conflicts peacefully:

> To achieve peace a leader would have to arise in the United States capable of meeting the explosive realities of Latin America halfway; Kennedy could still be this man. He still has the possibility of becoming, in the eyes of history, the greatest President of the United States, the leader who may at last understand that there can be coexistence between socialists and capitalists, even in the Americas. (1088)

As for shaping the future, the revolutionary leader favors Kennedy winning a second term and adds, "if you see him again, tell him that I'm willing to declare Goldwater my friend if it will guarantee Kennedy's reelection" (1088). Castro grants him having the potential to become a president of far-reaching historical import, "an even greater president than Lincoln" (1088).

Despite their opposing political beliefs and positions, Buckley and Mailer both shape the collective memory of Kennedy in a similar fashion. They give a positive take to his political record and import, savvy and maturity while they depict him not as an artificial figure, but as a human character with weaknesses and shortcomings.

Boston

> Kennedy started to speak, coughed, cleared his throat and began again. A girl at the rear of the crowd shouted, "Louder!" and he raised his voice with an effort, frowning. Some leader.
> It was a terrible speech. Terrible.[111]

When in 1946 he runs for public office for the first time, four Harvard friends mingle among the crowd at one of his street campaign appearances in Boston to have a look at the candidate: "Harvard's hat is in the ring [...] that sterling hero of Kula Golf, Beverly Hills and Miami Beach, John F. Kennedy, is running for the Congress of the United States" (326). What is known about him at this point is largely limited to press reports about his family and the medal he won for rescuing fellow naval comrades in the Pacific during World War II. One of the Harvard friends, Russell Currier, had met up with him during the war while being treated for a leg injury at Chelsea Naval Hospital where Kennedy was recovering from the aggravated back trouble he suffered after the Kula Golf rescue operation. Russ harbors some reserve and misgivings about the candidate as he is aware that Kennedy had acquired the nickname "Shafty" in the Navy after he managed to "leverage" himself up from a lower posting to the higher rank of patrol boat captain with the help of his influential father. Russ also denies him his attractive appearance: "I'm damned if *I* think he's so much on looks" (329). His friend George Virdon later recalls: "He needed a haircut and he was all skin and bones. He didn't look like any matinee idol to me" (330). Furthermore, Kennedy fails to impress as a speaker. Word of a disaster spreads through the crowd as he speaks. "A terrible speech," accuses Virdon:

> At one point he told a joke, a poor one, and nobody laughed. It was all vague generalities, fumbling, deadly dull [...] Kennedy kept pausing, his lips working, glancing around nervously. His hands made awkward, self conscious little chopping motions, which gave him a curious mechanical quality. It was all like something he'd tried to commit to memory, and hadn't quite. I could feel the mood of the crowd – flat, dutiful, unmoved, on the rim of disapproval. The faces of his own people around the car were rigid with disappointment ... He doesn't want to do this, I thought. (330)

The disappointment gives way as Kennedy manages to counter hecklers by making a case for his own agenda of reform, his personal commitment and the hopes of the younger generation for social change. Shouts such as "hey, that's pretty good, Shafty" (331) and "he's taking them" (332) mark a reversal in the crowd's reception. Initially reserved and critical, then somewhat accepting, it ultimately turns into full of approval: "He dropped his hands, and smiled. We were cheering, applauding wildly – it came out of us unbidden. This young man would speak for us" (333) – "'You know' Russ was saying, 'I think he means it'" (333).

Kennedy's generational appeal and his ability to rise up to challenges such as the one depicted in this episode from *The Last Convertible* are key features of Anton Myrer's fictionalization of John Kennedy. Like other similar elements they derive from Myrer's use of literary authentication, selection and attribution techniques. These mold recollections of the past and thus also shape the collective memory. Furthermore, they provide the parameters of a codex for an attempt at explaining the sense of self-exoneration prevalent among the members of Kennedy's generation in the book.

The novel retrospectively tells the story of five Kennedy contemporaries from the time they begin their studies together up until their 25th class reunion. It is this event that serves as the catalyst and the starting point for the reminiscing. Recalling the past turns into something more like probing scrutiny, however, when the grown children of the central characters confront their parents on such controversial topics as the economy's dominant role in society and the Vietnam War. The chief instigator is the young Ron Dalrymple, who questions the staunch George Virdon about his biological father in an effort to better understand his parents by learning the details of events and happenings that transpired many years before. The recollecting begins with the friends meeting for the first time in 1940 in Cambridge on the outskirts of Boston, describing the carefree college life of their early years at Harvard and then the abrupt transition to World War II and their experiences elsewhere. It continues into the post-war years, once again mostly in and around Boston, with their individual attempts to regain their bearings, pursue personal advancement and maintain their relationships with each another.

It turns out that Ron Jr. is Russ Currier's son from a first semester tryst. His mother, Chris Ferris, withholds news of his paternity from Russ, who is stationed in the Pacific during the pregnancy, due to his growing self-centeredness. She breaks off their relationship and instead marries another of the friends, Ron Dalrymple. It is as his wife that she gives birth to Russ's son, named Ron Jr. after his stepfather. Russ achieves the first break in his erratic writing career with a successful debut novel about his time in the Marines which brought him together with Kennedy in the military hospital. George Virdon marries his college girlfriend and remains the clique's perennial liaison figure. The Irish American Terrence Gilligan joins Kennedy's staff after returning home from serving as a prisoner of war and advances to the rank of advisor, but retreats from public life in bitterness after the assassination. Lastly, the Frenchman Jean des Barres parlays the war in Europe into university studies in Cambridge, but then drops out to return home and support Charles de Gaulle.

An automobile that is introduced to the quintet by des Barres early on, and later changes hands among them, comes to serve as their symbol of identification. They drive this car to nearby women's colleges, jazz concerts, football games, days at beach and "late-night necking parties under the maples" (10) listening to the music of Benny Goodman, Harry James and other music greats of the Big Band Era. George and the pregnant Chris survive an accident in the car, Russ returns with it to Boston from an unsuccessful stint as a screenwriter in Hollywood, and on the occasion of the 25th reunion it is nostalgically celebrated as a flamboyant group emblem: a well maintained, elegant companion to their shared experiences. The car, nicknamed "the Empress", is a 1938 Packard Super Eight Convertible in Berkshire green with gleaming chrome, a dignified shine and a voluptuous shape. George Virdon has it stored in his garage at this point and he sits in it for part of his discussion with Ron Jr. as he tries to graphically reconstruct the past for him with the help of old records and letters. His offer to give the car to Ron Jr. at the end of their talk is thankfully rejected. To the younger man, back from Vietnam, it represents a time in history with dreams for the future far different from those of his own generation.

Remarks such as "the convertible was freedom, it was youth, too – all our youth, all the youth we were ever to have, though we didn't know that then" (40) and "it was a car and yet it wasn't – it was a spaceship, a phaeton, a prairie wagon, a sloop running before the wind; it was everything we were and wanted to be" (40) make clear that right from the start "the Empress" symbolized for the students their approach to life in general: unencumbered exuberance, romanticized self-awareness and only vague aspirations for the future. Over the course of the novel this function expands to incorporate their whole age group. At the end when the news reports that Detroit will no longer manufacture open Cadillacs, George is led to declare the Packard the quintessential "last convertible" and young Ron rejects his offer to acquire it because "she was your chariot. She was for another time, another set of dreams" (531). "The Empress" has transformed into the symbol for an entire era in history and all those who lived it: the Kennedy Generation.

The book divides the experiences that George recounts into five chapters, each titled with a contemporary piece of music. The carefree vigor of their early college years bears the name of the swing song "Racing with the Moon". This is followed by the approaching shadow of uncertainty from the expanding war in Europe under the heading "I Don't Want to Walk without You" by Harry James. The third and middle chapter covering the succeeding years of World War II is named after the jazz-blues song "Don't Get Around Much Anymore". Here the form of the narrative abruptly changes. George Virdon interrupts his recollecting in the garage to methodically hand over to Ron Jr. one after the other and without comment a jumbled series of letters written by the friends from the front. Taken together they form a mosaic of war's turmoil. The dissolution of the group at this point is reflected in the fragmentation of the text and the absence of a coherent narrative voice. In the fourth and fifth chapters narrative continuity is restored. Efforts to reestablish prewar ties and make a fresh start after 1945 are titled "It's Been a Long, Long Time". The final chapter which tracks the personal ups and downs of the characters and those of the nation during the decades of the fifties and sixties is called "Serenade in Blue". The music progresses compositionally from the steady patterns of swing to the looser forms of jazz-blues and serenade. Thematically it evolves from lighthearted lust for life to nostalgic reminiscing. This musical development mirrors the group's self-awareness as it transforms from the stability and order of their time as young undergraduates to the upheavals and transitions of the war and post-war years.

Myrer blends a dichotomy into the symmetrical structure of the novel by integrating contemporary Kennedy references in different ways into the first and second half of the book. They are part of his pursuit of authentication.

The first two chapters include historical references to Kennedy. Actual events that closely correspond to the course of his life are frequently mentioned and used to repeatedly focus attention on him and his family. These include historical incidences which are synchronized with the plot to provide a timeline, such as in the following example for the year 1940:

> The music ended, the late news came on, British troops had captured Benghazi, the House had passed the Lend-Lease Bill, 260-165, FDR had named Winant to succeed Joseph Kennedy as Ambassador to Great Britain. (46)

The path of John Kennedy's life runs parallel to the lives of the other characters through to the second half of the novel, at which point they cross when he moves from the private sphere to the public arena in the 1946 election campaign in Boston. The Kennedy figure is brought closer to the other characters in step by step fashion until he finally interacts with them:

> Jack was moving toward us now, shaking hands rapidly and firmly, smiling that dazzling boyish smile, his tousled hair ruffled in the light breeze from off the river. I could hear his voice in the aspirant's ritual: "Thank you, I'll appreciate your support June 18th." (334)

It continues:

> He was very near us now; he caught sight of Russ, his eyes widened all at once." "Tolstoy!" I remember what Russ had told me about Jack's fondness for nicknames. "How's the gimpy leg?"
>
> "Sound as your aching back!" they laughed together […] "Nice going Shafty. I mean it."

"You're with me then? Coming over to the party of the future?"

"You know, I might just do that – against my better judgment." They laughed again, and Russ introduced us. Jack's grip was firm and quick, his eyes held on you with sharp interest; well no, it was more than that – you had the sense, for the single instant, that he was concerned with you and only you, in all this hooting, babbling crowd.

"You took them Jack," Terry was saying excitedly, "McNally, the whole Neville crew. You beat them at their own game! Terrific, terrific …"

That alert, intense, measuring look slipped back in Kennedy's face, "Gilligan," he said. (334)

The past is fictionalized by Myrer in a historically accurate manner. According to the criteria defined by Ina Schabert in her examination of historical narratives, the novel develops from a "fictional narrative in a historical setting"[112] in the first half to a "fictionalized course of historical events"[113] in the second half. Comparing the documentary records of the campaign for the 11th Congressional District seat in the House of Representatives with Myrer's literary version reveals how much the fictionalized Kennedy figure is actually drawn from historical context. His longtime companions Kenneth O'Donnell, David Powers and Joe McCarthy describe his reaction to provocation from the opposition in reporting the following incident:

One night in Charlestown a heckler tried to question him about this father's money. "I don't have to apologize for my father or any of the Kennedys," Jack said with his eyes blazing. "I'm running for Congress. Let's stick to that. If you want to talk to me about my family, I'll meet you outside."[114]

The corresponding passage in *The Last Convertible* reads:

"I don't have to apologize for my father or any of the Kennedys – Any of them!" Jack looked angry now, fighting mad; all the mechanical handchopping was gone. "I'm running for Congress from the 11th. You want to go after my father, Skip, I'll see you later." (332)

This exemplary comparison[115] with the biographical record of O'Donnell and the others shows the high degree of factual accuracy Myrer's depiction of Kennedy contains. It is the many historical references, the actual events from the era, the evocative undertones of the well-known songs and the highly distinctive automobiles that combine to create the novel's "fiction of historical experience"[116] and its intense impression of authenticity. This in turn serves to validate the defense of the war generation represented in *The Last Convertible* by George Virdon and his friends, who see themselves critically denounced by the baby boomers with their accusations of "fat profits turned into napalm" (513).

The identity of this age group and its destiny are called into question early on when military deployment severs their link with carefree freshmen hedonism. Russ Currier differentiates them from Hemingway's and Fitzgerald's Lost Generation of World War I when he says, "the Lost Generation, they called them.

Maybe they were. Well, we're the Ruptured Generation. Hung up between a wet dream and a bad dream" (147). Their war experiences leave deep and lasting scars. On returning home after being wounded or held prisoner their attempts to start over are met with the sobering realization that "we were still caught in attitudes fashioned before the war" (323). The insight that "the trouble was we hadn't been brought up to cope with reality – the reality under the reality, the one that mattered" (327) points to a case of stunted maturation, an unfinished process of initiation. While they experienced a great deal during the war, it wasn't a help to them afterwards when they faced making a fresh start. Rather, a persistent sense of disorientation sets in among the characters.

> There was time to do *everything* now, it seemed; the possibilities stretched before us – a lordly view from a mountain top...Yet there was a catch – we were still caught in attitudes fashioned before the war. Like a reformed gambler saddled with old debts we were frozen in the 1941 image of ourselves. Some weeks we'd bury ourselves in books and work through the night; then for no reason at all we'd leap into the Empress, race over to town, get roaring drunk and disorderly, hurling threats and insults at this new civilian order; and hours later find ourselves wobbling and wavering over some back country road. And for several days afterward we'd be sunk in boundless lassitude, hating Cambridge, America, life itself. (323)

Hopes and expectations of better things to come are voiced – "there were things in America that needed changing, and we were going to change them, too; come what may" (325) – but these sentiments remain vague and unfulfilled. In reaction to the nostalgic reminiscing at the 25th reunion the younger generation accuses their parents of retreating into the past instead of focusing on improving the present. They criticize the Vietnam War as a product of this attitude and pose questions that prompt critical introspection. Their parents respond with excuses that make reference to Kennedy's death and the feeling that his assassination caused many opportunities for accomplishing common goals to vanish. His generation feels robbed of the potential to achieve their own aspirations in the same way that he was thwarted in implementing his full program of change by his shortened time in office: "In an hour he was gone, and our generation's hour in the sun was gone too, for good – power had passed back to the shrewd, conniving old men of the 30's, before we'd even had a chance to get started" (485). George argues: "We've had to take the blame for your world – and we never quite held the real power. Only those thousand days of Camelot" (530).

The principal subject of the novel according to the author himself is the search for a common understanding between the generations. Anton Myrer, five years younger than John Kennedy, a New Englander from Worcester, Massachusetts, a Harvard graduate and a member of the Marine Corps during World War II, is aiming to create in *The Last Convertible* a convincing narrative reconstruction of the story of his generation:

> For a number of years, I wanted to tell a story about my World War II generation [...] At the same time, I wanted to say something about the youngsters coming of age in the 1960's. I returned to Harvard for the 25th anniversary of my class in 1969. This was in the midst of the campus unrest and the strong feelings against the Vietnam War – feelings which I shared with the kids. Some of them were the children of my classmates. [...] I felt a need to interpret our romantic generation to this embittered generation.[117]

His premise is that Kennedy's abbreviated term as President represents the deprived chances of his generation to pursue their dreams and, by extension, exonerates them from the shame of failure. To this end, the greater the impresssion of authenticity in the book, the more credible this premise appears. One way this is achieved is by maximizing similarity to a recognizable and widely accepted image of Kennedy through the use of literary authentication. The result provides Kennedy's generation a means for channeling its escapist feelings of self-forgiveness. Another way this is achieved is through an accurate depiction of the GI generation. Commentary such as "the story of our yesterdays" or "you will recognize yourself and all your friends"[118] proves this is the case in *The Last Convertible.* The ability of readers to relate to the book significantly contributed to its public appeal. The novel became a bestseller when first published in 1978 and was filmed as a popular mini-series for television in 1979 with Bruce Boxleitner in the role of George Virdon. At an emotional level, the sentiments evoked through the stirring effect of the well-known melodies and lyrics to contemporary songs and the overtly romantic imagery ("racing with the moon", "necking parties under the maples", "serenade in blue", etc.) help account for the warm public reception.

Because the author is caught up in the remembering process as an influencing factor himself, the image of Kennedy that appears in *The Last Convertible* is a self-serving one. But in addition to acting as a screen for projecting the author's intentions, the Kennedy figure also serves to reflect his whole generation's sense of self-awareness. Myrer's notion that his contemporaries are members of the "romantic generation" relates to this view of Kennedy. It is clearly apparent in the Camelot metaphor where the President is compared to the legendary King Arthur and Washington to his court from which the Knights of the Round Table disperse to do their good deeds.

Doubt and weakness have no role to play in such a conceptualization. Kennedy is never depicted as indecisive when faced with a conflict between what should and could be done or between his own views and those of others, even though his associates make note of this in their reporting of the 1946 election.[119] The novel does describe Kennedy's uneven first appearance on the political stage and his difficulties in rising to the challenge of the role, but the contrasts are used to highlight positive features of his character. There is no trace of him in the guise of a deeply conflicted political debutant, which for all intents and purposes was the case. That Kennedy aspired to pursue a career in publishing rather than politics, and only reluctantly heeded the call of family duty to assume the role of politician as successor to his older brother Joe Jr., is recounted by O'Donnell *et al.* They quote Kennedy making statements such as "sometimes we all have to do things we don't want to do" and "I'm just filling Joe's shoes. If he were alive, I'd never be in this."[120] Performance expectations that conflicted at least some of the time with his abilities and pushed him to his limit given his precarious physical condition turned into a burden for the election campaign. During a Bunker Hill parade he collapsed and "one afternoon, a veteran journalist found Jack in the back room of his Bellevue Hotel campaign headquarters weeping with fatigue and expressing disgust at what he had been forced into doing."[121] Such aspects are hinted at in *The Last Convertible* with George Virdon's remark about Kennedy's speech, "he doesn't want to do this" (330), but are not explored any further. The remark goes ignored. There is a selection process at work here whereby mainly certain widely accepted character traits of Kennedy are perpetuated and embellished.

Another example of this is his rapid transformation into a convincing speaker, which demonstrates an ability on his part to gain stature through his endeavors. What in reality was a slow, time-consuming process is reduced in the novel to the length of a single speech.

"Jack slowly developed a comfortable style," notes his biographer Michael O'Brian and refers to Kennedy's sister:

> Eunice Kennedy later recalled her brother being discouraged with the quality of his speeches, and her father's ever-present reassurance. "Many a night when he'd come over to see Daddy after a speech, he'd be feeling rather down, admitting that the speech hadn't really gone very well or believing that his delivery had put people in the front row fast asleep." But Joe encouraged him. "And then", Eunice continued, "and this was the key, father would go on to elicit from Jack what he thought he could change to make it better next time. I can still see the two of them sitting together, analyzing the entire speech and talking about the pace of delivery to see where it had worked and where it had gone wrong."[122]

And David Burner writes:

> Jack's father was a great help; for a weak speech the son first received praise from the elder Kennedy; then, no longer defensive, the candidate was told his faults, which Joe had carefully complied from listeners in the audience. Jack's public speaking improved.[123]

Condensing a lengthy process of self-improvement to the short span of just one public appearance, in a broader sense, attributes to him a superior potential for personal growth and greatly enhanced overall stature.

A similar attribution technique for upgrading his standing as a candidate – and by extension implied to apply to his entire generation – can be found in the positive political implications of his youthfulness. This factor was repeatedly held against him in the campaign on the grounds that he lacked experience and maturity. During the election race for the House of Representatives those of his age saw him as a spokesperson for themselves, the younger generation, "the contrast was perfect – old pols and young reformer [...] a new generation on the march" (322), tied to a feeling of hope: "He's going to wipe it clean – all the old dirty deals, the graft, the bullshit" (336). His candidacy is presented as an opportunity for a generational change and an end to the existing political status quo tainted by the widespread but mistrusted system of the party machine and its bosses. The reality at the time was that access to key political and administrative positions, in particular at the regional and municipal levels, were controlled by this powerful political machinery.

The political machine developed from organizational structures established in the 19th century which progressively expanded over time and proved repeatedly resistant to reform. Its focus came to center on urban areas where non-protestants and non-Anglo Saxon immigrant groups struggled to assert themselves against the dominant class of White Anglo Saxon Protestants (WASPs). Help and support were offered to newly arriving immigrants by family members and others from their homeland already established and familiar with the social and cultural environment of the community. Certain individuals strengthened their role as bosses by addressing issues such as housing, employment, childcare, leisure pursuits and neighborhood disputes in a manner that conformed to the respected traditions of the homeland. This in turn permitted them to continually expand the reach of their influence and the sphere of dependency linked to them. The result was a mutual support network, extending at times to patronage, which was quickly discovered to be a useful tool for acquiring election votes. The respective local party organizations increasingly served to turn the system of socio-ethnic loyalty into an apparatus for acquiring and retaining political power, i.e. the political machine. "The earliest urban political machines were dominated by the Irish who arrived first in the nineteenth-century city and brought a tradition of basing their politics on personal loyalty."[124] They introduced "the classic Irish route of politics."[125]

Local politics in mid-twentieth century Boston with its large Irish-immigrant population was largely controlled by such party bosses. Office racketeering and corruption were commonplace in the city administration, shortcomings which are repudiated as the "graft", "old, dirty deals" and "bullshit" of the old-style political guard by the novel's characters when they return from the war disillusioned and skeptical. Hence they see their spokesperson in the younger man running for office. Kennedy's youthfulness distinguishes him from the "old pols" and makes him a blameless candidate. In this way, youthfulness suggests not just the more standard associations of vigor, determination, optimism, etc., but also a brand new political understanding connoted in the thought "this young man would speak for us" (333). After Kennedy's death George observes: "Power had passed back to the shrewd, conniving old men of the 30s" (485).

The Last Convertible contains both parallels and differences to Vance Bourjaily's *The man who knew Kennedy.* Bourjaily, who like Myrer was a Kennedy contemporary, attempted to document his generation's relationship with Kennedy in literary form as early as 1964. His spokesmen are also Harvard graduates. The first-person narrator Barney James, like George Virdon in Myrer's novel, reflects on events and developments during his youth and time as a student, the war and the post-war period. These conjure up the past, creating "an evocation of the memories of a whole generation, from the 10c Wings cigarettes of the Depression to the melodies of forgotten songs and long silenced dance-bands."[126] He shared his most formative experiences with the book's main character, his best friend from childhood Dave Doremus. Dave is "the man who knew Kennedy" and it is from Dave's perspective that Kennedy's depiction initially proceeds. It is Barney as narrator who explains all of this and mulls it over, however, which provides the book with a double perspective on Kennedy. This is augmented with reference to Sinclair Lewis' 1928 novel *The Man Who Knew Coolidge*. While there are similarities with *The Last Convertible*, there is no attempt at self-exoneration in *The man who knew Kennedy.* Instead, the novel poses a somewhat satirical self-criticism of this generation whereby thinking back about Kennedy exposes actual memories set side by side with exploitatively misappropriated ones.

Like Lewis' better known works *Main Street* (1920) and *Babbitt* (1922), *The Man Who Knew Coolidge* is a satire of America's provincial middle class, a sardonic portrayal of the smugness and petty bourgeois narrow-mindedness that has come to be known as babbittry. "The man who knew Coolidge" is Lowell Schmaltz, an ambitious businessman in the fictional mid-western town of Zenith, where *Babbitt* is also set. Schmaltz is a braggart and a bigmouth, notoriously at pains to glorify himself through rambling, self-aggrandizing monologues on topics of all sorts – an anti-hero. He defines himself chiefly through his supposed acquaintance with President Calvin Coolidge, whom he purportedly knows from their time together at Amherst College. His tales of their encounters there vary depending on the circumstance. The same is true for a surprise visit his family makes to the White House. Schmaltz fails to encounter the president personally, but this does not hinder him in the least from recounting conversations with Coolidge's secretary as worldly exchanges with "Cal" himself.

Barney James serves as the reverse image of Lowell Schmaltz and George Babbitt in *The man who knew Kennedy.* Originally from mid-western St. Louis, he marries into a New England family that owns a company he meanwhile proudly manages. He is an affectionate father to his children and devotes his free time to hobbies such as woodworking, reading Shakespeare, listening to music, sailing and bird watching. The reader develops "an instant, easy rapport"[127] with him as a reliable narrator, a role which the enigmatic Dave Doremus cannot credibly fill. His reputation is tarnished by questionable business dealings and his self-destructive relationship with a drug-addicted jazz singer casts doubt on the soundness of his judgment. The juxtaposition of main character and narrator in *The man who knew Kennedy* draws a parallel in this respect to F. Scott Fitzgerald's *The Great Gatsby.*

Barney James read Lewis' *The Man Who Knew Coolidge* when he was fourteen, but remembers little more than the title. He borrows a copy of the book in the hope that rereading it might furnish a link to his friend Dave: "When the title bobbed up in my head I thought I'd see if there was some connection."[128] He spontaneously associates him with Kennedy: "Dave was among my friends, the man who knew Kennedy" (3).

The family backgrounds and early lives of Dave Doremus and John Kennedy turn out to share similarities and overlappings. Both of their fathers held important positions under Franklin D. Roosevelt, including advisor to the President, and in the case of Joseph P. Kennedy Sr. Ambassador to London. From a young age their sons win attention for their cleverness, intelligence and charm, qualities which earn them recognition as peer leaders from their fellow students. Barney James suspects that they met each other while boys:

> The Doremus family used to spend their summers on Cape Cod, too. They weren't as important in the government, or rich, but I guess they saw the Kennedys sometimes. Dave resented the Kennedy boys, he says, but then he got to know … John Kennedy. A little better. (31)

The similarity of their paths in life continues during World War II, which results in them meeting in a marine hospital just like Kennedy and Russ Currier in *The Last Convertible*: "A couple of wounded men in bathrobes" (78). Doremus reflects:

> It was sort of magical meeting a Kennedy in the hospital. They'd always been glamorous people to me, and here was one getting bossed around by Navy nurses, just like me. He had one of the worst cases of malaria they'd ever seen – I don't think he weighed 130 pounds. (145)

The relationship is marked by Dave's feelings of unspoken rivalry. This took root in his childhood when he bemoaned the less influential position of his father under Roosevelt compared to Joseph P. Kennedy Sr. He also admitted "there was some direct rivalry in the summer sailing", "and envy of the money" (147). In the clinic, he consequently finds important the reassurance that there was nothing patronizing about Kennedy's attitude towards him:

> I was impressed by him […] I don't think it's wrong to say he thought pretty well of me. He must have because I stopped feeling challenged by him, and I wouldn't have if there'd been anything patronizing in the way he talked to me. (145)

Kennedy's diminished physical condition and status have an equalizing effect. Doremus sees him more as "one thin and anguished man" (80) than as an opponent.

As time goes by, however, the old competitive feelings resurface. While Myrer in his book makes use of the 1946 congressional elections, Bourjaily instead chooses the next step in Kennedy's political career, the 1952 elections when he wins a seat in the Senate for the Democrats. Doremus suffers defeat as a Republican congressional candidate in this election ending his political aspirations. From this point on the lives of Kennedy and Doremus proceed to diverge ever further. Kennedy's rise is contrasted with Doremus's downfall, a fact that Dave ultimately acknowledges: "I think he grew and grew and grew, like Roosevelt. I think that … persistent growing's what it takes to make a great man" (147). With this remark he accedes to Kennedy an ability to transform goals and challenges into personal growth.

The years to come for Doremus, contrary to all earlier optimistic expectations, are filled with professional and personal crises to which he finally succumbs. With his drug-addicted second wife, to whom he returns despite marrying a third woman, he commits suicide. A former classmate's description of him as "one half faun, the other half gargoyle" (15) proves to be prescient. An *amour fou* in his private life contributes to his demise, just as it does with Jay Gatsby. As his downfall advances, his friends retrospectively ask him what induced him to run for a seat in Congress in 1952 as a Republican given his background which includes his father's success in the Democratic Party, his own civic-minded political calling and the similarities he sees in himself to Kennedy. "'John F. Kennedy,' Dave said, and let that lie around on the table for a moment" (144). He further acknowledges that "I was a Democrat any time in my life, up to a couple of days before I became a Republican candidate" (144). He saw himself faced with two alternatives – either supporting Kennedy as a promising Democrat and following him to Washington as a member of his staff, or winning a House seat on his own either on the back of the Republican Party's national strength under Eisenhower or with the next opportunity to come along for the Democrats:

> Well, I didn't want to just get a job down there. And maybe I didn't want to wait my turn. Kennedy was going to win his Senate seat without me, of course; but suppose he didn't? It was going to be a big Eisenhower sweep nationally. That was pretty clear. So call the practical thing a standoff – wait my turn with the Democrats, and build some local strength. Or try it with Ike, and hope he'd carry me in. (146)

He opts to enter the race as a Republican and loses – the first in what eventually becomes a long series of miscalculations on his part. Although his younger years seemed to hold such promise for the future, he never does manage to find his calling in life and sets out instead on an unrelenting downward spiral. Doremus fails to recognize, however, that the true reasons for his demise are his self-debasement, his opportunistic attitude, his impatience and his erring strategic calculation. He instead blames Kennedy. This failure to acknowledge personal inadequacy is a theme that again correlates with *The Last Convertible.*

The musings about Kennedy are related and expounded upon by Dave's friend Barney James, in particular through the reminiscing of this first-person narrator. In most cases these thoughts are triggered by songs which bring back memories and, in some instances, sentimental feelings as well. The jazz classic "Skylark" by Johnny Mercer and Hoagy Carmichael serves as a theme song throughout the novel. When the narrator reverts to reflecting on the past during these passages the point of view is shifted from that of an external observer to the introspection of a narrated monologue.

The trigger for one such sequence has Barney softly playing "Skylark" on the piano one sleepless night. The song brings back memories of his student years intertwined with thoughts of Kennedy: "I started thinking, then, about Dave talking about Kennedy" (157). At first he wonders if he might be somewhat envious of this relationship, "for some reason – begrudged Dave's having known him" (157). But, as similarly portrayed in *The Last Convertible,* he accedes to his generation's embracement of Kennedy: "That was it: I knew Kennedy. We all knew Kennedy, didn't we? He went to college and the war with all of us" (157). Then he empathizes with Dave, who feels challenged and made uneasy by Kennedy. He asks himself if he, too, wouldn't have reacted with such mixed emotions in the face of the high esteem attributed to Kennedy as a peer leader with self-confident mannerisms and a privileged background.

> Wasn't Kennedy the particular upperclassman in the fraternity, poised and cool but not unfriendly. It was the poise that made a freshman feel uncomfortably awed by him; and the grooming. What'd the guy own, a barbershop? [...] To think the petty thought: that look is bought, with money, starting young and rich with orthodontists and saltwater summers, to build what goes under the cashmeres and the camelhairs. You were better off in college for not thinking things like that? (157-8)

As he continues to play "Skylark" the song's choruses are overlaid with contemplations about Kennedy:

> *Second chorus*: Wasn't Kennedy the upperclassman about whom you asked yourself, does he know I'm here? And so, trying to imitate the quickness and accuracy with which he could keep the senior table laughing when he wanted to, you tried some of your own, jejeune stuff on him once. And he didn't even cut you down, in reply, just frowned for a second and then smiled and went on with his interrupted conversation. (158)

His mid-western origins initially heighten his sense of inferiority, but then this feeling subsides:

> *Skylark. Third chorus.* He was what you hated in the fraternity and the college, coming east from St. Nowhere on the Mississippi, with your baseball glove and your old taped spikes,

everything you hated when you hated it. And everything you liked, eastern, when you liked it. Everything you loved and hated in New England. Fair; always fair, when you could get his attention. (158)

This perceived lack of self-assurance and presence of mind is reflected in the restless way that Barney plays the piano; "I played a run, some chords, got into another key and back to the melody, up tempo" (158).

An analogy can be drawn between the functions of the altered choruses of "Skylark" and the chorus in classical drama. The ancient chorus often either assumes the voice of an idealized spectator (or the audience as a whole), or addresses the audience directly as an aid to understanding the work more fully. The opportunity the reader is given to relate to what Barney says parallels this first case. The tempo of these narrated monologue passages is slower compared to the other parts of the text which occur with a time-lapse. This is because the narrating time is identical to the narrated time itself. Barney's train of thought and the act of reading it occur simultaneously. The process of reading and experiencing this synchrony induces the reader to identify with Barney and his ambivalent reflections on Kennedy. The second person singular "you" can refer to Barney James addressing himself in this mental dialogue. It might, however, also refer to him directly addressing the reader in the same way the classical chorus is used in the second case. The rhetorical questions and answers ("Wasn't Kennedy [...]?", "Wasn't Kennedy [...]?", "He was what you hated [...]") further help to guide the reader's sympathies in this direction. Kennedy's generation is targeted first and foremost, but beyond that a broader readership as well, drawn to the sense of a shared mind-set.

The characters also use Kennedy for their own purposes, going so far as to appropriate him in an attempt to define themselves. In this respect, the broadly satirical overtones of Bourjaily's criticism of his generation differ in comparison to *The Last Convertible* but draw parallels to *The Man Who Knew Coolidge*. Like Lewis he sets out to expose weaknesses in both the individual and in society as a whole. He starts by making the following observation:

For a couple of years before and after the assassination of John F. Kennedy you'd find yourself talking with someone who had served with him in the war, who'd shaken his hand or been acquainted with some member of his family.[129]

This phenomenon occurs primarily as the result of thinking back about Kennedy and outwardly reflects an inner sense of belonging to his world. But *The man who knew Kennedy* also sheds light on the difficulties that surface when this attitude is critically scrutinized.

An insignificant incident is transformed to take on greater purported meaning when some positive personal attribute is seen as stemming from a brief encounter. Other than a few chance meetings there is, in fact, no real close acquaintance or extended contact which ties Doremus to Kennedy, as he admits when talking to Barney's wife:

> "I haven't seen any of the Kennedys for eight or ten years. Not since I first ran."
> "You ran too?"
> "For the House. For the other party. 1952. And got beat." (78)

He was as Republican in this election to the same minimal degree that he is actually acquainted with Kennedy. Nevertheless, just like Lowell Schmaltz, he defines a part of his identity based on having met the President. Linguistically this is already expressed in the title of the book, which consists of a defining relative clause without a comma between "*The man*" and "*who knew Kennedy* [/*Coolidge*]".

The subject turns generational when Dave's third wife, Connie, also stakes her claim and declares "so we've all known Kennedy" (163). Casting reservations about her age, Barney counters by saying "I'd have thought you were a little young". "I was ten years younger than John F. Kennedy," insists Connie, "you going to throw me out of the game?" (163). She rightly detects an age "game" at play with respect to such (self) appropriated Kennedy credentials. Barney's wife also takes part:

> "When I was a little girl," Helen said, "I went to a dance as the guest of a little boy who was just starting in Choate. And somewhere in the mountaintops there was a boy named Kennedy, a senior, who was pointed out to me. So I might have seen him." (211)

Pointing up the irony in "the game" requires the pill-popping and alcohol addicted Art LaBranche, a dropout from this social class with a peripheral view from the sidelines:

> "Johnny Fitz. One time, one time inna Boston Garden, Mrs. Barney,..."
> "Yes," Helen was being pleasant and kind. "Yes, Art?"
> "It was schoolboy hockey. Played for champs inna Boston Garden, and I was MVP. Most Valuable...anything. Anything you want. Imagine that? And he was senator, I guess. And pinned a medal on most valuable me..." (210)

As with Art's medal, so it is with much of this Kennedy comradeship: it serves as a flattering status enhancer, an extra dividend so to speak, stemming from a completely arbitrary source that is no longer verifiable, i.e. "anything you want." The absence of any real meaning in such behavior is metaphorically illustrated and emphasized through repetition of the ironic "most valuable". Revealing here the use put to having met or having wanted to meet Kennedy exposes an intrinsic artificiality, and along with it the empty posturing of the "game" to partake in the aura, prestige and membership of this select group.

The unveiling of such weaknesses creates satire, but one that is more didactical in purpose and ironic in character than bitingly sharp. The moral overtone derives from the criticism that can be applied in a general way to the common tendency in human nature to enhance personal status with extraneous virtue. This provides the novel with a measure of universality. The irony is underscored in that the satire does not stop short of the narrator. The satirical implications go undetected by him as well, just as in *The Man Who Knew Coolidge*. The participants in the exposed game are not only other members of Kennedy's generation, but also Barney himself, who goes so far as to flatly disavow any trace of satire in *The man who knew Kennedy*: "As for Mr. Lewis: [...] The things we see around us aren't really jolly enough to satirize" (5). For the most part he does not register the criticism directed at the attitude and behavior of his peers such as Dave Doremus. Consequently, there is no change in the way he approaches and deciphers his friend such as might be expected from him having read Lewis' novel. He manages to go no further than the trace of irony detectable in his comment "you owe something in this life to the people who help you define yourself" (27) and the ostensible notion that Dave Doremus was destroyed by his second wife.

Barney James reflects back not only on Dave Doremus but also on Kennedy in connection with *The Man Who Knew Coolidge,* providing the reader a comparison of the two presidents. He starts off in agreement with the poor critical acclaim accorded Lewis' novel by referring to it as "really a bad little book" and to its protagonist Lowell Schmaltz as "a real offensive idiot" (4). The reliability of the narrator is strengthened by these initial comments and the two novels are juxtaposed for comparison. "Things are totally inverted" (4), says Barney and he cites the following as an example. Firstly:

> Lewis's sonar was a pretty precise piece of equipment. I'm perfectly convinced when he picks up Lowell Schmatz summing up Coolidge: "Maybe he isn't what my daughter would call 'ritzy'... he may not shoot off a lot of fireworks, but you know what he is? HE'S SAFE." (4)

Then comes the contrast:

> John Kennedy was just exactly what *my* daughter, Mary Bliss James, would have called so "ritzy" if she'd used the word; I think the fifth-grade word just then was "neato." And as for shooting off a lot of fireworks? And did we care to elect a man who was, in Schmaltz's capitals, "SAFE?" (4)

And shortly thereafter: "Mr. Coolidge died, for example, old and at home, neither honored nor dishonored; no one paid much attention. That's not the way John Kennedy went" (5).

Kennedy and Coolidge both came from New England, represented Massachusetts first in the House and then in the Senate in Washington, and are considered to have been popular Presidents. The public standing of both men, however, contrasts significantly. Unlike Kennedy, Coolidge was an extremely shy man of few words which earned him the nickname "Silent Cal". He made the "politics of silence"[130] a distinctive feature of his term in office by focusing more on administration than leadership. He espoused the values and goals of the business world including its philosophy of free-enterprise (caricatured in the character sketch of Lowell Schmaltz), governed in a non-interventionist manner, showed little interest in foreign affairs and made few efforts domestically on behalf of the needy such as the African Americans. Quite to the contrary, he permitted thousands of Klu Klux Klan members to march through the streets of Washington in 1925. By comparison, Kennedy governed more demonstratively in both domestic and foreign affairs, responded with greater active intervention when required and projected far more charisma as President.

The Kennedy in *The man who knew Kennedy* conforms with this favorable comparison. The intertextuality of the novels and the narrator's repeated reflections on Lewis's creative process metafictionally draw attention to the act of writing narratives as such. This emphasizes that Bourjaily's "totally inverted" novel about Kennedy, when placed alongside *The Man Who Knew Coolidge,* serves as a positive reverse image which preserves the intended satire. Bourjaily avails himself of this satire for his dedication at the front of the book: "This novel is dedicated, inevitably, to the memory of President John F. Kennedy, but it is an oblique sort of monument."

The novels by Bourjaily and Myrer each present a nostalgic look back at perceived shortcomings following Kennedy's death from their respective timeframes in the present. This is conveyed in *The Last Convertible* in particular through the criticism voiced by the children, and in *The man who knew Kennedy* through the example of Dave Doremus's misery. His widow, Connie, crystallizes this in saying, "it's been ghosts all the way, Barney. Ever since the assassination hasn't it" (162). Kennedy serves in these recollections not just as the embodiment of better times gone by, but also as a representative and a role model for a new generation – for which purpose he is endowed early on with a range of winning attributes such as personal growth. Attempting to bask in the glow of these attributes as compensation for one's own personal deficits implies the existence of a certain Kennedy mystique, which in itself here again constitutes another such characteristic. Thus both novels form an "oblique sort of memory" contributing to and serving as part of the collective memory.

Excursion

Attempts to portray individuals have a long-standing tradition in art and literature. They are found between the poles of individualization and type-casting, representation and interpretation, vilification and idealization. Whether it is at all possible to paint an adequate and communicable image of a person is one of the questions Donald Barthelme addresses in "Robert Kennedy Saved From Drowning", a text consisting of a sequence of 24 fragments varying in length, in which different facets of Kennedy are presented, as in "*K. Reading the Newspaper*" for example:

> His reactions are impossible to catalogue. Often he will find a note that amuses him endlessly, some anecdote involving, say, a fireman who has propelled his apparatus at record-breaking speed to the wrong address. These small stories are clipped, carried about in a pocket, to be produced at appropriate moments for the pleasure of friends. Other manifestations please him less. An account of an earthquake in Chile, with its thousands of dead and homeless, may depress him for weeks. He memorizes the terrible statistics, quoting them everywhere and saying, with a grave look "We must do something." Important actions often follow, sometimes within a matter of hours. (On the other hand, these two kinds of responses may be, on a given day, inexplicably reversed.) The more trivial aspects of the daily itemization are skipped. While reading, he maintains a rapid drumming of his fingertips on the desktop. He receives twelve newspapers, but of these, only four are regarded as serious.[131]

In the other sections of the text, further partial views are provided: "*K. at His Desk*", "*K. Penetrated With Sadness*", "*Described by Secretaries*", "*Dress*", "*A Friend Comments: K.'s Aloneness*", "*Gallery-Going*", "*K. Puzzled by His Children*", "*With Young People*", and "*K. Saved From Drowning*". They show Kennedy defusing a critical situation with a telephone call, reading to his children, making himself a drink, dreaming, how matter-of-factly he dresses himself, him visiting somebody in a hospital, how radio music touches him emotionally, his concerned reaction upon hearing news, his view of his active role as helper; Kennedy in his office, in the bar, in a boat, in a restaurant, at an exhibition, travelling and so on. Diverse types of information are strung together without any transition.

Among them in a text fragment about the renowned photographic artist, Youssuf Karsh, famous for his portraits of celebrities, is a reference to the topic of portraiture:

> *Karsh of Ottawa*
> "We sent a man to Karsh of Ottawa and told him that we admired his work very much. Especially, I don't know, the Churchill thing and, you know, the Hemingway thing, and all that.

> And we told him we wanted to set up a sitting for K. sometime in June, if that would be convenient for him, and he said yes, that was okay, June was okay, and where did we want to have it shot, there or in New York or where. Well, that was a problem because we didn't know exactly what K.'s schedule would be for June, it was up in the air, so we tentatively said New York around the fifteenth. And he said, that was okay, he could do that. And he wanted to know how much time he could have, and we said, well, how much time do you need? And he said he didn't know, it varied from sitter to sitter. He said some people were very restless and that made it difficult to get just the right shot. He said there was one shot in each sitting that was, you know, the key shot, the right one. He said he'd have to see, when the time came." (39-40)

The people who speak in the text fragments besides Kennedy himself can either be deduced from the context, are occasionally announced ("friend", "former teacher", "secretaries"), and sometimes remain undisclosed. A continuous narrative does not emerge and the sequence of texts parts neither forms a coherent plot nor does it follow any linearity. Their arrangement appears arbitrary, a principle of composition that reflects Barthelme's view of the world and is thematically relevant.

In well-known remarks he characterized his fragmentary poetics as "emphasizing the juxtapositions, the stranger disjunctions, that are part of [the] everyday experience of modern life."[132] They confirm his perception of a world that in its totality cannot be comprehended. As Peter Freese puts it:

> This fundamental view, which Barthelme shares with other so-called black humorists such as John Barth and Thomas Pynchon, Joseph Heller and Terry Southern, Bruce Jay Friedman and Kurt Vonnegut, leads him to consequently reject the conventional short story form with a beginning, middle and end, for how could a fragmented and meaningless world be depicted by a coherent and purposeful plot.[133]

Toward the end of the narrative, in the penultimate vignette, the structural characteristics of the entire text are once again mirrored and linked to the overarching theme:

> *He Discusses the French Writer, Poulet*
> "For Poulet, it is not enough to speak of seizing the moment. It is rather a question of, and I quote, 'recognizing in the instant which lives and dies, which surges out of nothingness and which ends in dream, an intensity and depth of significance which ordinarily attaches only to the whole of existence.' What Poulet is describing is neither an ethic nor a prescription but rather what he has discovered in the work of Marivaux. Poulet has taken up the Marivaudian canon and squeezed it with both hands to discover the essence of what may be called the Marivaudian being, what Poulet in fact calls the Marivaudian being. The Marivaudian being is, according to Poulet, a pastless futureless man, born anew at every instant. The instants are points which organize themselves into a line, but what is important is the instant, not the line. The Marivaudian being has in a sense no history. Nothing follows from what has gone before. He is constantly surprised. He cannot predict his own reaction to events. He is constantly being overtaken by events. A condition of breathlessness and dazzlement surrounds him. In consequence he exists in a certain freshness which seems, if I may say so, very desirable. This freshness Poulet, quoting Marivaux, describes very well." (45-6)

The characterization of a "Marivaudian being" as "born anew at every instant," and the subsequent comment, "the instants are points which organize themselves into a line, but what is important is the instant, not the line," are revealing in two regards. Firstly, with the subordination of linearity, a self-referential compositional image of the entire text emerges, namely a metaphor for the principle which creates, irrespective of prioritized continuity, a totality from the sequencing of individual parts, which defy closure as well as rigid order. It is a characteristic of this type of fiction "to assert disorder as an aspect of being."[134] In this way, the underlying structural principle reveals itself in a partial text. Secondly, the definition of "Marivaudian being" with regard to the portrait theme refers to the dubious nature of the wish to pin down a constantly changing and always differently perceived personality – "born anew at every instant" – in a text or picture.

Beyond the compositional principle of fragmentation and paratactic montage, the postmodern short circuit is readily discernible. Text parts 1 to 23 are presented with a documentary character, in the form of descriptions, reports, commentaries, excerpts from interviews, etc. When asked about his sources because of the high degree of "precision and insight of the piece",[135] by Kennedy biographer, Arthur Schlesinger, Barthelme claimed his reproduction of reality was "the result of watching television and reading the *New York Times*"[136] and the episode in which Kennedy visits an exhibition in "*Gallery-Going*" as authentic: "I happened to be in the gallery, when he came in with a group."[137] In contrast to reproductions of that kind, the final text fragment is clearly different:

> *K. Saved from Drowning*
> K. in the water. His flat black hat, his black cape, his sword are on the shore. He retains his mask. His hands beat the surface of the water which tears and rips about him. The white foam, the green depths. I throw a line, the coils leaping out over the surface of the water. He has missed it. No, it appears that he has it. His right hand (sword arm) grasps the line that I have thrown him. I am on the bank, the rope wound round my waist, braced against a rock. K. now has both hands on the line. I pull him out of the water. He stands now on the bank, gasping. "Thank you." (46-47)

In the context of the complete narrative, separate levels of being, the factual and the imaginary, are connected to one another, fact and fiction are short-circuited, thus dissolving the borderline between reality and imagination, between world and art. The result is a hybrid approach to Kennedy comprised of documentary snapshots and non-documentary supplementation.

This collage technique can also be found in art, for example in the combine paintings of Robert Rauschenberg, whose montage technique has long since become a widespread principle of composition. Various elements of different ways of refering to reality, both paintings and drawings as artifacts and photographs as quotes from reality, are included in the painting together with real objects, mixed with each other and thus short-circuited. The components are not subject to any apparent principle of order, but simply strung together, just like Barthelme's text segments. Different materials are put together to create one perception, which seeks to involve the addressee in the process of creative activity: "It is all put together in the head,"[138] says Rauschenberg of the intended effect of this method.

Barthelme follows this tradition and puts it into practice here. He began this text collage shortly after ending his work as managing editor of the magazine *Location*, which was dedicated to the relationship between the visual arts and literature and was published by Larry Rivers and Robert Rauschenberg among others. The author wrote four novels, a children's book and over a hundred short works of fiction. "His natural narrative space was the short story, if *story* is the right word for those often plotless marvels of which he published some seven volumes over 20 years," writes John Barth in his appraisal entitled "Thinking Man's Minimalist: Honoring Donald Barthelme".[139] In Wayne Stengels attempt to categorize Barthelme's short fiction, the text at hand is assigned to the group of "art stories", of which self-reflection is the common denominator: "Some ask from what materials contemporary art can be formed; others question whether human beings are the proper subject matter for art."[140]

Barthelme is skeptical about the latter question as hinted in the notion of the "Marivaudian being". His text offers the reader a heterogeneous compilation of disparate personality facets and a variety of perspectives, but does not capture the personality. A kaleidoscope of snap shots is presented, but not a representative "key shot", which typically is also not available from Karsh as photo portraitist. The text is in this way a seemingly contradictory "portrait of a man who is ultimately unknowable."[141] Statements such as "his reactions are impossible to catalogue" or "he's very hard to get to know" (40) underline this. These comments echo not only the problem of really understanding a (public) person but particularly the uncertainty as to whether "the ultimate mystery and privacy of the individual"[142] are to be respected, and they reveal the "futility of conclusively defining an individual temperament."[143] Such self-restricting tendencies illuminate the limits of the medium in which one is working. Lois Gordon's observation, "the mystery remains, both about Kennedy and about what words can mean,"[144] aims at exactly this intersection between the plot level and the metalevel (if the initial "K." is understood as reference to everyman as in Kafka and Brecht, this leads immediately to further possibilities of generalization).

Self-restriction motivated by respect for the personality and insight into the limitations on the power of textual expression cause Barthelme to abstain from trying to achieve a concluding, fixed portrait, the idea of a final sameness in which the character or essence of a person is revealed. This does not, however, stand in the way of a personal approach to the historic figure. The text uses available facts in the

The Profile

Barthelme's contribution shows the questionable nature of attempts at textual portrayal. A synopsis of the most disparate information and perspectives cannot do justice to the personality or even reveal it. Thus in the narratives discussed here, only a partial visualization of John Kennedy can be accomplished. The evocation and perpetuation of familiar Kennedyana (appearance, Harvard, rocking chair, etc.) can hardly be surprising, but what is notable is that certain profile features emerge against the background of the existing JFK image. In some cases these correspond with American myths, which provide a foundation for the present and reflect national self-images. In some cases they are critical of the present or they revise myths. Furthermore they explain the special status of Kennedy in the collective memory and the function of literature in connection with this.

The fictionalizations are, as has been shown in the preceding analyses, intended to preserve the greatest possible agreement between the perception of the historical figure and the literary depiction. The increased plausibility arising from this and the illusion of experiencing history that is conveyed to the reader have already been discussed. In light of Winfried Fluck's concept of fiction as a "strategy for mastering a world of experience that has become problematic,"[145] in that its unsatisfying nature is compensated for with a "symbolic transformation"[146] dispensing with such a fictional reattribution or reshaping of Kennedy is indicative that he is not viewed as problematic or requiring modification. This implies a fundamental acceptance of the man and his politics on the literary side.

However, a conceptualization and formulation of an allegiance to reality for the purpose of considering the contours of the profile and their cultural context must be qualified here and is subject to reservations. As DeLillo suggests, perceptions located between the real person and the image established and distributed via media are hardly distinguishable. He refers to this intricate network of relationships, already in place during Kennedy's lifetime, in *Libra* through the description of the reception of Kennedy at Love Field Airport: "He looked like himself, like photographs." Person and images can no longer be truly kept apart. In the subsequent course of decades of such interference, these reciprocal superimpositions and transmissions have become increasingly diverse and more decisive for the forming of his image in the collective memory.

Five profile lines generated in the texts play a part in this development. The first arises from the ability to grow and mature. Kennedy's initial steps in politics are described as not very promising and during his candidacy for a seat in the House of Representatives his performance in the Boston street campaign shows little promise of success. He does not cut a good figure as he is deemed: a poor speaker with erratic gestures, weak points and hardly a winning appearance, who is even pulled to pieces by members of his own generation despite their shared experiences and objectives. Later he makes a better impresssion, demonstrates the necessary positive qualities and is capable of the tasks and able to convince. This growth pattern already established in the early years continues. At the beginning of his presidency, inexperienced as he was and trusting in the expertise of the secret service and the military, he takes over the operation in the Bay of Pigs. From this he learns to counter such pressures with skepticism and steadfastness, and to weigh his decisions more carefully. These are insights that enable him to act in a manner appropriate to the situation during the missile crisis of the following year, in the face of considerable pressure, and to assert successful crisis management with the aim of avoiding a nuclear war. The depictions of this are narratives of growth, examples of the realization of a traditional American self-conceptualization.

Its roots extend back to Puritanical didacticism in the New England of the 17th century, the purpose of which was not only to convey Calvinistic teachings and train its preachers, but by taking a view of man as reprobate, it also served in his improvement. This goal was secularized in the 18th century by proponents of the Enlightenment like Benjamin Franklin, and thus liberated from its Puritanical burden. Improvement and self-improvement have endured to the present day as standard objectives of the American educational system and to some extent developed into a collective self-image.

The American narrative tradition of initiation literature has contributed to this and has been exemplified again and again by such varied heroes as Mark Twain's Huckleberry Finn, Ernest Hemingway's Nick Adams, Jerome D. Salinger's Holden Caulfield and Harper Lee's heroine Jean Louise Finch, to name a few, all of whom undergo a maturing process in narratives of growth. They impact upon and continue an American myth and auto-stereotype.

As in the Kennedy literature analyzed here, his personal development process has also been emphasized in biographies about him:

> The saga typically begins with Kennedy's childhood experiences of illness, injury, and sibling rivalry that ostensibly challenged him to develop a strong character, prevented him from becoming weak or spoiled, and equipped him with sensitivity to the misfortunes of those without his privileges. The pattern of growth allegedly continued into Kennedy's early manhood, his heroic exploits in the South Pacific and the deaths of his brother Joe and his sister Kathleen further maturing him. According to his biographers, such a process was also

evident in JFK's political career. As a congressman, he started out as a loyal adherent of the isolationist views of his father and condemned the internationalist foreign policies of FDR and Truman. But travel abroad and contact with liberal intellectuals impressed him with the need for American involvement abroad and made him more sympathetic to the aspirations of the Third World.[147]

Thomas Brown traces "the pattern of growth" for Kennedy's presidency and emphasizes its archetypal character: "the posthumous versions of Kennedy's life bear similarities to the archetypal myth of the hero who acquires spiritual insight through suffering and experience."[148] This can be expanded to the narratives. Brown refers to Joseph Campbell, who, as a student of Carl Gustav Jung, continued his comparative mythology research. According to the fundamental principles of Jung's psychology, unconscious, deeply anchored, and primal human ideas, referred to as archetypes, and originating from common fundamental experiences of mankind, are found in myths in a pronounced form. Residing in the "collective unconscious", they form homologous thought structures, which in turn form cognitive dominants in the consciousness of the individual. He includes the archetype of the maturing hero among these deep structures, not least because the experience of personality development is universal, as is the hope held out for maturity acquired with increasing age. The linking of Kennedy with this archetype has two effects. Due to their appeal to the "collective unconscious", such human archetypes in literary texts create a connection between the respective figure and the readers on the basis of shared elementary experiences. Secondly, with respect to the collective memory, a process of myth-formation emerges by way of the archetypal motif of growth and the maturing process, as well as the related singling out of the individual case from the temporal and spatial coordinates of its existence.

A second profile feature arises from the presentation of Kennedy in a position of governmental responsibility, in this case from the reenactment and revitalization of the myth of virtuous power, which can also be traced back to an American tradition of thought, and which contributes to the nation's perception of itself.

In the first half of the 17th century, when the Puritan immigrants saw themselves faced with the task of self-administration in the wilderness of New England, they established the principles for this based upon the Bible. After the Pilgrim Fathers, separatists from the English state church, had founded Plymouth Plantation in 1620 to the southeast of present day Boston, another group followed in 1630, which had not broken with the Anglican Church but was instead attempting to reform it with the model of an exemplary community in the New World. Before they turned to establishing such a settlement, the Massachusetts Bay Colony, to the north of Plymouth Plantation, their leader, John Winthrop, described his idea of self-organization based on virtue in his "A Model of Christian Charity" sermon. In the conclusion he urged his followers to succeed in this project, because all eyes are turned to this experiment as to "a city upon a hill".[149] The awareness of the exemplary character of their community was a core element of Puritan colonization and flowed into the tradition of American exceptionalism, itself a myth, according to which the nation is understood as "qualitatively different,"[150] but not necessarily "better" in comparison to others. As a consequence of New England developing into the pre-eminent region, it left its mark on the later nation, especially with respect to this mindset. Toward the end of the 18th century, this American exceptionalism was then organized and institutionalized with the founding of a self-administering political system independent of European political realities. The democratically constituted United States has seen itself as a model of (virtuous) self-government, which has deepened and perpetuated the idea of otherness, and with it the myth of virtuous power in the national consciousness. This collective self-image found expression in the 19th century in the idea of Manifest Destiny, the mission of spreading democratic civilization, and saw itself confirmed when the U.S. became the destination of countless immigrants, who left the oppressive conditions of the Old World behind them and saw their chosen home in the new one, with political, religious, and economic self-determination, and the promise of a better future:

> Americans have seen themselves not simply as the exemplary bearers of universal civic and political values and thus a witness to the world of the validity of these values, but as a people uniquely qualified by history and circumstance to fulfill and embody them.[151]

In the process, and persisting into the early 20th century, a touchstone of American politics shaped by George Washington, Alexander Hamilton, James Monroe, and later by Andrew Jackson, was to protect the interests, the distinctiveness, and the virtues of the United States with a policy of political self-limitation, with isolationism. However, Woodrow Wilson later on interpreted the exceptionalist tradition and the Manifest Destiny ideology as a global policy task involving the peaceful spreading and continuing development of democracy and the securing of peace. "It was Wilson's dream after 1918 to put American virtue at the service and leadership of a new world order that would ensure the spread of democracy and the onset of perpetual peace."[152] Henry Kissinger states: "Wilsonianism presumes that America is possessed of an exceptional nature expressed in unrivaled virtue and unrivaled power."[153]

The political constellations changed with the Second World War, as did the manner of dealing with this myth as a consequence. During the Cold War, the United States, on the basis of its hegemony in the West, assumed the task of helping to rebuild the so-called "Free World" and defending it against expansive and undemocratic communism. An ideological confrontation dominated by block thinking thus arose, which was often characterized by a juxtaposition of good and evil. "Yet such black-and-white dichotomization," according to John Kane, "caused an unfortunate deformation of the myth of virtuous power. In the foreign policy consensus that emerged after World War II, that myth congealed into politically inflexible anticommunism."[154]

In Buckley and Mailer it is precisely this deterioration of the myth that Kennedy counteracts, in that he both personally overcomes the conflict-laden, dichotomous world view typical of the time and begins to implement this new perspective in concrete policy. Through him, the primal American myth of virtuous power, which has withstood the challenges and transformations of American culture until the middle of the 20th century, and the continued existence of which is now endangered in the context of the Cold War, is revitalized. The myth is reenacted and continued in political virtues, such as self-discipline and restraint in the use of power. Kennedy links both of its components, while after him American foreign policy vacillates back and forth between them as between two different poles (for example, Jimmy Carter's focus on human rights in favor of virtue and George W. Bush's Iraq policy veering in the opposite direction). Kennedy's combination of the different elements of the myth not only prevents its continuing disintegration, but also the questioning of a key aspect of the national self-image. His inclusion in the ranks of the custodians of the myth of virtuous power has a retroactive myth-making effect on himself.

The third profile characteristc originates from the convergence of the collective and (Kennedy's) individual myth of youthfulness and its connotations, which are especially prominent in *The Last Convertible* and *The Man Who Knew Kennedy*. "The 'eternally young' Kennedy […] has become a symbol of how many Americans have traditionally seen their country."[155] Not only because it cannot yet look back on a long history, but also due to the special circumstances of its origins as a nation, America sees itself as possessing properties of youthfulness, such as the courage to change and reorganize, and of progressivity, dynamism and independence; attributes that are also ascribed to Kennedy in the texts.

Paul Kirk, at that time the federal chairman of the Democrats, remembers Kennedy's presidency as being a time of "the country feeling young and good about itself."[156] In fact, Kennedy, as a representative of the young generation, not only differs from the politicians of the old stripe in terms of age, but also in terms of bearing and gesture, thinking and objectives. What links him and his generation is, on the one hand, bitterness resulting from the experience of war, along with mistrust of the political establishment, and a feeling of having the right to help reshape in the face of the need for the renewal of the social order on the other. He is distinguished as much by the fact that his first candidacy for political office was launched independently of the prevailing patronage mechanisms, without running with the machine, as he is by his aversion to the political rhetoric and behavior of the old style: "The candidate was by nature reserved, skeptical, and averse to schmaltz; his reticence in campaigning was a departure from backslapping, glad-handling Boston politics."[157] In concrete political work he also demonstrates independence from party opportunism and notables, and even his outward appearance is commented on regularly: "more than a few congressmen grumbled at the casual, sloppy, and unmatched clothes he wore on the House Floor."[158] Political observers consider his successful application for the nomination as the presidential candidate of the Democratic Party as the start of a generational change; former president Harry Truman publicly expresses doubts as to the readiness for office of the then 43-year old, given his youthfulness. Theodore H. White on the Democratic National Convention of 1960 in Los Angeles:

> One way or another a convention is an assembly of older men, averaging in age over fifty, some of whom boast of unbroken attendance at nominations that reach back to the time of the nomination of Woodrow Wilson. Almost as much as the national Congress, the delegates (at both conventions) preserve the continuity of American politics. It was these older men who first reflected what was happening; it was visible in the various shades of melancholy on their countenances: one could see drifting through the lobbies of the Biltmore such former powers as James Farley, Tommy Corcoran, Scott Lucas, Claude Pepper – but they were powerless now, ghosts at a banquet over which they had presided. [...] Of all the master figures of the past of the Democratic Party, only Harry Truman was absent. By instinct, knowing that time had passed him by, he would not expose himself to this tide of youth.[159]

Beginning with the slogan "John F. Kennedy – leader of the new generation" from the election campaign of 1946 until his presidency commencing fourteen years later, the generation and youthfulness themes developed into a symbol of political renewal. Kennedy himself commented on his victory in intimate circles with the remark, "never again will anyone from [Adlai] Stevenson's generation be president. I think the establishment resents our youth as much as anything else."[160]

The change from the oldest holder of office to the youngest officially took place at the inauguration ceremony in January 1961. In his speech Kennedy addressed the idea of rejuvenation at the pinnacle of the country, which had been spread by the media and brought to the consciousness of the public through a variety of discussions of his relative youthfulness, in order now to project its connotations across generations onto the nation as a whole. Robert Frost, the first representative of literature and art to be present at a presidential inauguration, emphasized the youthfulness of the new president in the opening lines of the poem written for this occasion. This theme attained such prominence that it appeared advisable to also add signs of maturity to the transition to a younger generation, including the message of renewal symbolized by it. Rhetorical references to the Constitution and to the Founding Fathers in the inaugural address can be viewed as such, as can the connection of objectives with the fundamental values of the nation and the pioneer virtues of the frontier generations of the 19th century, as well as the appearance of the venerable poet by the side of the young politician. With an average age of 47 years, his cabinet was ten years younger than that of the Eisenhower administration and remains the youngest in the last century. The president was not only six years younger than his later successor Reagan; he also took office twenty years earlier.

Beyond rhetoric, his self-representation serves the purpose of targeted image and media management. Photos were distributed showing him as a young father with his small children, even engaging in athletic activity, but not playing golf which could have been associated with Eisenhower and his generation.

Because the image of the youthful Kennedy, representing a change of generation, has not been diluted by a process of wear or aging due to his early death, it endures and solidifies in the collective memory – with the help of literature.

While the living Kennedy embodied positive national auto-stereotypes, his death is presented as the start of a time characterized as negative. This has emerged as a specific feature of his assassination and the subsequent era, and is associated with phenomena of dissolution. In DeLillo's novel, the assassination as such plays just as important a role as the loss of Kennedy, which is in the foreground for Brautigan, Updike, Morris and Manchester. Kennedy appears as an agent of solidarity, the absence of which then results in disintegration – "cultural decomposition" is the corresponding diagnosis of W.J. Rorabaugh for the period after Kennedy.[161] This outlines a fourth profile aspect, which brings home the problems of the years of its emergence, the time after Kennedy's death in Dallas.

Kennedy sought a mandate for change in the election campaign of 1960 with his program of the New Frontier and the appeal, "it's time America started moving again".[162] During his nomination for the Democratic presidential candidacy in July 1960 in Los Angeles, he presented his agenda, characterized by a sense of departure, to the party and the public. Terms like "change"[163], "challenge"[164], and "courage"[165] are keywords here. In connection with the formative experience of expanding the boundaries of settlement westward in the 19th century, the mission now is to depart for new frontiers with the same pioneering spirit. These frontiers take on the form of "*un*charted areas of science and space, *un*solved problems of peace and war, *un*conquered pockets of ignorance and prejudice, *un*answered questions of poverty and surplus [emphasis mine]."[166] In rhetorical terms, what is still to be achieved is emphasized by the repetition of the prefix "un", and this homoiarkton is complemented by repetitive suffixes in an homioteleuton foregrounded with alliteration and asyndetons: "the times demand inven*tion*, innova*tion*, imagina*tion* [emphasis mine]."[167] With this rhetoric of change balancing new tasks with an outlook for success, Kennedy also conveys the courage to accept the challenges. This is because departure simultaneously means change. It also requires the giving up of a seemingly secure *status quo* for a process of restructuring that is fraught with uncertainty and risk.[168] Following the successful election, he was also able to create a climate of optimism and an acceptance for the implementation of his management of change for the coming social, political, and cultural transformations. In terms of domestic politics, the challenges were many and included the overcoming of segregation, the improvement of the economic situation and the living conditions of the low-income population, as well as the reorganization of the cities, the restructuring of the family in the wake of the sexual revolution and the redefining of the role of women within the framework of employment and feminism, dealing with the consequences of demographic changes in favor of the baby boomers, and with cultural developments:

> The Beat writers Jack Kerouac and Allen Ginsberg, both of whom gained increasing respectability in the early sixties, the great songwriter Bob Dylan, and the pop artists Roy Lichtenstein and Andy Warhol collectively destroyed an already decayed mainstream culture that was largely left over from the late nineteenth century.[169]

Moreover, in the area of foreign policy, of primary importance was the defusing of the Cold War with its regional trouble spots, and the limitation of the arms race, as well as the conceptualization of a new policy for dealing with the so-called "Third World".

In the process of change, Kennedy became the figurehead of a new beginning, reflecting the hopes of not only a new generation, but of a broad majority across generations. And not only of Americans, but of the people of many nations. His murder resulted in a sudden rupture. "A promising time ended as the assassination in Dallas killed both a popular president and many of the hopes he represented."[170] The transformation successfully commenced was abruptly terminated. As implementation stagnated, in some cases solutions crucial to advancing developments remained uncompleted. Kennedy's successors were unable to ensure continuity in this regard and following the murder of the president, the mood of the country changed. A lack of hope and optimism became disappointment and frustration which led to the radicalization of reform movements in the late 1960s and increasing eruptions of violence. There was serious racial unrest, such as that seen in the Watts district of Los Angeles in 1965. In addition violent confrontations between Black Panthers and the enforcers of public order, the division of the country by the Vietnam War, often accompanied by violence, police brutality against protesting young people at the Democratic convention of 1968 in Chicago, as well as the militant coup attempts of the Weatherman Underground, could all be experienced on the television screen at home, which inscribed these events deep into the collective memory. The solidarity of a phase of renewal borne by optimism under Kennedy made way for the disintegration of a "more frenzied, often raucous, and even violent era that followed,"[171] leading to "the terrible violence and chaos of the late sixties."[172] Kennedy's death, with the loss of a bearer of hope and reformer, also meant the loss of an agent of coherence and stability – qualities that are not only emphasized in the postmodern narratives but also in their more traditional counterparts.

Myth-shaping profile elements exist beside myth-revising traits. These involve the posthumously created and oft-cited Camelot myth and the facets of his operative image that refer to the vitality of the president. The Camelot comparison dates back to then popular musical *Camelot*, created by the successful duo of Alan Jay Lerner and Frederick Loewe. The show premiered in 1960 on Broadway with Julie Andrews and Richard Burton in the leading roles.[173] As an adaptation of Terence H. White's version of the Arthur legend in *The Once and Future King*, it tells of the legendary king and the Knights of the Round Table at his court in Camelot, who have dedicated themselves to the struggle for justice. The record of the soundtrack was America's topselling album for more than sixty weeks and the composer Loewe played several of the songs at a White House dinner in May 1963. They were among Kennedy's favorites, especially the last piece, in which Arthur dubs young Tom of Warwick a knight in the field of battle and commissions him the task of passing on the noble, chivalrous code and the ideals of Camelot to future generations:

> Don't let it be forgot
> That once there was a spot,
> For one brief, shining moment
> That was known as Camelot.[174]

Following the funeral of her husband, Jackie Kennedy proposed an article in *Life*, that compared Camelot with the Kennedy administration. "For President Kennedy: An Epilogue" in the December 1963 issue met with strong public fervor against the background of general mourning. The Camelot metaphor has persisted since, although Kennedy's staff discount it in his name. His secretary, Evelyn Lincoln, presumes that he himself would not have thought much of the comparison: "You know what [the President] would have said about it – 'Oh, not *that* trash!'"[175] His close adviser, Lawrence O'Brien, also distances himself from the retroactive myth-formation: "I don't think there was a Camelot,"[176] he points out, and then adds in sober reflection:

> But really what it was all about was hard work, seven days a week, every waking hour, to try to accomplish the presidency and reach the objectives of his program [...] If at any time Camelot existed, it eluded me."[177]

And Arthur Schlesinger writes:

> Had those of us around the President ever proposed such a fancy, no one would have kidded us more swiftly or decisively than Kennedy himself. Certainly J.F.K. listened to the Camelot record late at night. So did we all. This did not implicate us in its plot.[178]

Regardless of this, "the fancy" is upheld in countless publications, most clearly in William Manchester's *One Brief Shining Moment: Remembering Kennedy* published in 1983 and in Robert Dallek, Hugh Sidey, *et al. The Kennedy Mystique: Creating Camelot* from 2006. "Touched by the intimacy of death and mourning most Americans forged a special bond to the dead leader," according to Thomas Reeves on the Camelot effect. He goes on to describe the main component of it as follows:

> A literature of adulation, the likes of which the nation had not experienced since the death of Lincoln, soon burst into print. JFK became a sort of superman, a legendary figure who presided over Camelot.[179]

The literary conceptions do not follow this line. Kennedy is not presented as a "superman", but instead much more as a human being. He leaves an overall impression that is in fact not reminiscent of a "matinee idol". Beginning in the early years and throughout his presidency, he suffers from health problems, such as his complaints following spinal surgery, his "degenerating discs", and Addison's disease (an adrenal cortical insufficiency, requiring permanent medication with cortisone, and which is fatal when left untreated). He experiences insecurity and conflicts, demonstrates both positive qualities and weaknesses, and makes mistakes. As it is no superman that is shown here a partial reversal of the myth occurs. In the face of his vulnerable health[180], this results in an alteration of the part of his official image as a powerful and vital politician associated with *vigor*. Yet, this does not lead to a diminishment in any sense.

A comparable development characterizes the representations of Lincoln: while in the second half of the 19th century chiefly hagiographical, myth-making modes prevailed, no such adulatory efforts are evident in the 20th century. Walt Whitman still elevates the murdered president in the Lincoln poems of the later editions of *Leaves of Grass* in a cosmically exuberant and idealizing fashion, while Carl Sandburg's 1926 biography *The Prairie Years* and the 1939 sequel *The War Years* increasingly place the focus on the human side, behind the myth. Gore Vidal, in his 1984 novel *Lincoln*, offers even more consistent access, in that he presents the man with physical and psychological instabilities, with digestion problems, fatalistic moods, with laudanum cocktails to combat his depressive episodes, with poorly fitting and often disorderly clothing; a man who is vulnerable and who suffers the conflicts and dissensions of politics, but who also acts in a coolly calculating and assertive manner, and who is also not afraid to use undemocratic means to preserve the unity of the nation. However, this also does not diminish his reputation or his achievements. In a time in which the Lincoln Memorial in Washington is no longer primarily meant as a reminder of the person, but instead symbolizes the rightfulness of waging the Civil War, Lincoln is no longer treated in the literature as a monument. Instead, his humanness is emphasized.

This makes his struggles and experiences more comprehensible and honors his achievements as something fought for and won. "His [Vidal's] Lincoln is not a debunked portrait by any means," Joyce Carol Oates thus justifyably claims, "and as the novel runs its course, he emerges as a truly outstanding man."[181] His achievements and importance appear as all the more worthy of respect, because they were won not only against external, but also internal adversity.

A comparable effect also applies to Kennedy, when his human sides, including his role as a "connoisseur of the sexual game,"[182] are not neglected. As a consequence the JFK-Camelot myth is not promoted and perpetuated and Kennedy is not stylized as a slick heroic stereotype, that loses sight of him as a human being. It prevents him from becoming what Peter Goldman feared in a *Newsweek* edition dedicated to Kennedy: "a man lost in his legend."[183]

While most of the profile lines sketched up to now have a collective function of establishing and reinsuring identity, his death, as was further demonstrated, was a disruptive event that ushered in a new era. It shook the collective identity which initiated a process of change, a search for a new identity, which at first passed through a phase of "decomposition" at the cultural level. The assassination represents such a deep disruption that it resulted in a national trauma as defined by the findings of trauma research (according to which individual psychological categories can also be applied to the collective), and as the journalist Walter Cronkite anticipated at an early date: "there's no question, the assassination was a serious blow to our national psyche [...] the trauma was very deep."[184] One of the effects of traumatization is that the memory of the triggering event is not allowed entry into the explicit memory, as less stressful, everyday experiences are, because, according to Cathy Caruth, "the trauma is the confrontation with an event that, in its unexpectedness or horror, cannot be placed within the schemes of prior knowledge."[185] It only finds access to the implicit memory. Here it cannot be called up and controlled according to the normal mode, as Bessel van der Kolk and Onno van der Hart state. Instead "it becomes dissociated from conscious awareness and voluntary control."[186] It is therefore remembered differently, and in a way that is often accompanied by phenomena of repetition. "Indeed repetition is the definitive symptom of what Freud called 'traumatic neurosis,' whether that symptom is manifested as flash-backs, recurring nightmares, compulsive behavioral reenactments, or other psychic disturbances."[187] The recurring preoccupation with Kennedy, "that American culture remembers Kennedy ad infinitum,"[188] can thus be understood as an indication of a trauma suffered with the death of Kennedy, making a kind of Freudian "working through" necessary. "Certain events," writes Roger Bechtel on the basis of a drama and film-based analysis, "do seem to have the capacity to do profound psychic damage across a wide swath of communities and people, and the Kennedy assassination certainly seems to bear this out."[189] He concludes “that the assassination of President John Kennedy provoked collective trauma on a national scale.”[190]

Such a view provides a socio-psychological attempt at explaining the continuing treatments of Kennedy as they are undertaken in literature, especially for the peak of contributions revolving around his death. The texts can be understood as forms of expression following a national trauma, the experiences of which occupy an unusual status in the collective memory. Here they are stored in the implicit rather than the explicit part, and thus separated from conscious access, they are dissociated. The narrativization of the unsettling content is necessary in order to overcome the resulting impairment of normal memory activity, because “traumatic experiences are the unassimilated scraps of overwhelming experiences, which need to be integrated with existing mental schemes, and be transformed into narrative language.”[191] According to this, literature carries out a therapeutic task in its narrativization. It assists in a process of regeneration, leading from dissociation to the integration of the difficult event:

> The trauma […] requires integration, both for the sake of testimony and for the sake of cure. Transformation of trauma into narrative memory that allows the story to be verbalized and communicated, to be integrated into one’s own, and others’ knowledge of the past.[192]

The enduring preoccupation with the subject suggests that this process has not yet been completed.

The various contours outlined here converge to reveal a composite profile of Kennedy. But it is not adulatory. Correspondences with the existing and especially with the officially created image of the president observed on the literary side are not suitable as indicators of an elevating mode, as they also correspond with reality. This could generally be shown with the profile features and can at this point be further bolstered with the example of the fulfillment of the myth of virtuous power.

Besides through careful media management, Kennedy’s operative image manifests itself and is demonstrated in, among other things, his actions and his rhetoric. The latter is expressed in an exemplary fashion with regard to foreign policy in his American University Address held in Washington in June 1963. In this, the most important geopolitical speech of his presidency, he takes experiences and insights gained from the Cuba Crisis into account and develops his “strategy of peace”.[193] Rejecting the idea of a *Pax Americana,* he promotes objectives such as the avoidance of “confrontations which bring an adversary to a choice of either humiliating retreat or nuclear war” (286), as well as the limitation of the armaments race, the overcoming of mutual distrust, and finally “just and genuine peace” (286). He calls for a change in perspective as the prerequisite for peace at home and around the world, especially between the opponents of the Cold War. Antithetical expressions for conflicts and problems account for realities, but are held together by recurring figures of speech that emphasize similarity, so that, in keeping with a rhetorical principle that takes its evocativeness from the incorporation of the contradictory into the coinciding and the connective, the commonalities which become recognizable through the new way of looking at things, outweigh the differences. The intention and the appeal of the speech are thus reflected in its rhetoric and realized in a way that rushes ahead and points the way, by which means rhetorical design insinuates the practicability of the thing strived for. Catchy forms of this process are chiastic phrases like "let us not be blind to our differences – but let us also direct attention to our common interests" (286). Kennedy himself also increasingly assumes another perspective and breaks through the ideologically fixed, dichotomous modes of perception of the Cold War in that he places the defensive precautions of the Soviet Union within the framework of its experiences in the Second World War:

> At least twenty million lost their lives. Countless millions of homes or farms were burned or sacked. A third of the nation's territory [...] was turned into a wasteland – a loss equivalent to the devastation of this country east of Chicago. (285)

He also abandons the accentuated role of the president several times when, reinforcing the rapport with his audience, he stresses commonalities in his role as a human being and a father: "in the final analysis, our most common basic link is that we all inhabit this small planet. We all breathe the same air. We all cherish our children's future. And we are all mortal" (286). In this speech Kennedy reframes otherness into alikeness and opposition into congruity.

Among the initially achieved concrete implementations in the spirit of his peace rhetoric (or deténte rhetoric) are the Nuclear Test Ban Treaty and the reorientation of the NATO doctrine of massive retaliation based on the deterrent of a nuclear counterstrike to flexible response, in order that, in the event of a conflict, it would be possible to react in graduated steps without the immediate compulsion to escalate. Also of note is the support of less developed countries through the Peace Corps and cooperative ventures like the inter-American Alliance for Progress.

On the subject of the course of action Kennedy took during the confrontation Roger Hilsman writes in *The Cuban Missile Crisis: The Struggle Over Policy* from a historical-political perspective:

> The keynote of the U.S. response was flexibility and self-disciplined restraint – a graduated effort that avoided trying to achieve too much and that stopped short of confronting its adversary with stark and imperative choices.
>
> Out of this basic policy flowed the precedents – restraint in the use of power; flexibility in developing a solution; the pacing of events to give the other side time to think and so to obviate "spasm reactions"; [...] the deliberate regard for precedent and the effect of present actions on the longer-range future; and, finally the relevance of moral integrity to that longer-range future.[194]

In his study, *The Cuban Missile Crisis,* historian Mark J. White evaluates the decisive phase of the face-off:

> During the second week of the crisis Kennedy's overall performance was superb [...] as the crisis progressed he became more flexible and conciliatory, more earnest in his efforts to avoid war. He resisted the temptation to react forcibly to seemingly intolerable Soviet provocations.[195]

Even in his Kennedy-critical, psycho-historical *A Question of Character: A Life of John F. Kennedy*, Thomas Reeves concedes:

> A large number of powerful men in Washington, including ExCom members, Pentagon officials, and Congressional leaders, would have speedily invaded Cuba and dared the Soviets to engage in nuclear war in an effort to establish our predominance in global power. No doubt because of lessons learned from the Bay of Pigs fiasco (Bobby said later that "we didn't have an exercise with the army in which they didn't screw up"), and surely for deeper reasons concerning the fate of the human race, Jack chose to resist this course of action. [...] Kennedy was not reckless. Indeed, he demonstrated the ability to seek counsel, make decisions, and maintain reasonable control of an enormously complex crisis to the benefit of all. [196]

The list could be continued, so that the historian Robert Dallek can speak of "almost universal praise for his [Kennedy's] restraint and accommodation in the missile crisis".[197] With reference to the related overcoming of the prevailing dichotomous world view, also emphasized by the literature for the broader context of the Cold War, William E. Leuchtenburg confirms "that Kennedy, after several false starts, moved American foreign policy, to some degree, away from the bipolar assumptions of the Cold War."[198]

Because profile content concurring with the operative image is supported by such historical-political findings, such correspondence is not suited as indication of an elevating approach, which would also oppose the myth-revising elements.

In summary it can be said that representations of Kennedy converge in an overarching, coherent profile. This coexists, competes and interacts with historical, political, individual and other evocations of Kennedy in the collective memory. With respect to the formation of a JFK myth, promoting and inhibiting elements are both found, while most of the attributes of the literary profile correspond with foundational American myths and auto-stereotypes. The linking of political reality and the inherited individual and collective self-understanding thereby offers possibilities for identification and conveys the perception of finding oneself in Kennedy and his politics. A large part of his popularity addressed at the beginning, as well as his significance for the national identity, can thus be explained. It makes the epochal disruptiveness and the traumatizing effect of the assassination comprehensible, in light of which the enduring preoccupation with Kennedy as part of a coping process becomes clear, with most treatments dealing with the assassination. The dissolution phenomena documented here turn out to be stress symptoms relating to the loss or collapse of orientation. A transition to a healthy coming to terms position can be seen in the attempt to keep the memory of Kennedy alive. That his fictionalization does not result in compensatory reattribution, but more in a pronouncing of traits, suggests a fundamental affirmation and confirmation of person and policy, which corresponds with the observation that no controversial profile is incorporated into the collective memory. However, there is also no indication of adulatory visualization. The narratives steer a middle course between hagiographic and revisionist memorialization. In the end, Kennedy's own adage, entirely in agreement with Barthelme, applies to any attempts to approach him, as well as to their cumulative effect: "Each man remains something of an enigma."[199]

Beyond Narrative

The contributions of drama and poetry can be integrated into the literary profile, even if these two genres are less differentiated in their presentations of Kennedy. The poems are more individual and more reflective, while the plays show more of a societal concern and are more provocative.

Barbara Garson's piece *MacBird!* and Wendy MacLeod's *The House of Yes* primarily deal with the trauma of the assassination. *MacBird!* also looks at the cultural disintegration after Kennedy's death, something that is not possible for MacLeod's drama due to its being written later in 1997.

Several lawyers declared a staging of *Macbird!* to be impossible[200] and theaters refused to perform it. The printer in charge, and later a filmmaker, Jay Rosenblatt boycotted Off Broadway productions with his unwillingness to provide programs for such "tasteless nonsense"[201]. Publishers declined to publish it. The liberal *New Yorker's* stance saw it reject an advertizing order for a play for the first time in its 42-year history. A performance of *MacBird!* was forbidden in London. FBI boss Hoover commented:

> Lawlessness, unbridled vulgarity, obscenity, blasphemy, perversion and public desecration of every sacred and just symbol [will] destroy the nation [...] We should be alarmed when widespread recognition and monetary awards go to a person who writes a satirical piece of trash which maliciously defames the President of our country and insinuates he murdered his predecessor.[202]

He went on to compare the author with "offbeat dolts whose ability is measured only by how they can dip their poisonous pens into the pots of blasphemy, filth and falsehood."[203]

MacBird! is an adaptation of Shakespeare's *Macbeth*. The personnel and the plot are thus for the most part prescribed: encouraged by the ambiguous prophecy of three witches and driven by his wife, Macbeth murders the rightful King Duncan in order to succeed him, but in the end falls victim to the followers of the slain leader, who free the country from the tyranny of the usurper and name Duncan's sons Malcolm and Donalbain as the legitimate heirs to the throne. In Garson's version, the murderer of the king is called MacBird, and is presented as a fictional portrayal of the president of the time, Kennedy's successsor Lyndon Johnson. Motivated by the prophecy of the witches and animated by his ambitious wife, modelled on Lady Bird Johnson, he kills the revered Ken O'Dunc. As is clear, he is meant to be equated with John Kennedy, with the evocative name refering to his Irish background. In addition to the suggestive names, unambiguous illustrations ensure the identification of those represented, so that President Johnson is unequivocally fictionalized as Kennedy's murderer.

The play begins with the National Convention of the Democratic Party in Los Angeles (here in 1960 Kennedy won the nomination as the presidential candidate and offered to contest the election together with his competitor Johnson as his running mate and vice-presidential candidate). MacBird hears the prophecy of the witches which initiates his murder plans, immediately before receiving O'Dunc's offer:

1st WITCH: All hail MacBird! All hail the Senate's leader!
2nd WITCH: All hail MacBird, Vice President thou art!
3rd WITCH: All hail MacBird, that shall be President! (I, 2, 10)[204]

The plans of the MacBirds to help fulfil the rest of the prophecy develop once the party convention and the successful election have brought about the first part of the prediction. As Duncan's stay with Macbeth in Inverness seals his doom, Ken O'Dunc is killed during his visit to Texas, the home state of the MacBirds.

The murder is staged using details based on the Warren Report:

(*A downtown street. The backdrop is a line drawing showing a six story building toward the left, a grassy hill and a railroad overpass to the right. A crowd lines the street, standing at the front of the stage with their backs to the audience so that the parade route is imagined to be between the crowd and the backdrop* […] *Right after the shot is heard, a projector throws an X in a sixth floor window of a building, trajectory lines extend from the building to the side walk, lettering appears, reading "Grassy Knoll", "Railroad Overpass", etc. In this way the backdrop becomes a newspaper diagram of the assassination scene.*)

1st VOICE: Oh no!
2nd VOICE: Can't be!
3rd VOICE: They've shot the President!
5th VOICE: Oh, piteous sight!
1st VOICE: Oh, noble Ken O'Dunc!
2nd VOICE: Oh, woeful scene! (I, 7, 1-23)

This reenactment of the assassination can be understood as "traumatic repetition."[205] However, doubt as to the official version of events is already expressed through the name given in the imprint of the self-publishing company which brought *MacBird!* out, "Grassy Knoll Press". Named after the hill to the front and right of the open presidential vehicle, it offers a nod to the conspiracy theories that state assassins were situated there placing Kennedy in a crossfire.

The Macbeth-Johnson and Inverness-Dallas analogies presented, whereby Kennedy's successor in office is accused of having carried out a secret *coup d'état*, serve as spectacular vehicles for an attempt at exerciseing political influence. It is not the *Macbeth* parody and travesty, or the Shakespeare pastiche, with borrowings from *Hamlet*, *Richard II*, *Julius Caesar* and *Macbeth* that are positioned in the foreground, but instead political satire as a contribution to the political discourse of the election year of 1968.

By way of his fictional counterpart, a stupid and ruthless, lance-swinging, power-mad figure in kilt and Scottish bonnet, President Johnson is held up to ridicule. MacBird's common Texan idiom contrasts meaningfully with the mostly iambic, often blankverse language of other figures (whereby the tension between Shakespeare's original and its adaptation to 20th century America flashes through). In addition to the authorship of the conspiracy, in the following dialogue MacBird is also credited with decreeing a sham investigation to be carried out by the Earl of Warren, who is not difficult to equate with the real figure:

MACBIRD: My predecessor's death has grieved the nation.
EARL: Indeed he was beloved.
MACBIRD: (*Gruffly*) Indeed, quite right.
Now some folks whose wits are crazed with grief
Still seek a villain, chase a phantom foe.
Although the killer's killed, they cannot rest.
And I desire to set their minds at ease.
EARL: Small doubts still flit like fleas throughout the nation.
MACBIRD: That's why I'd like a full investigation,
Conducted by man of such repute
That we may put an end to all these doubts.
That man is you.
EARL: Oh, cursed spite
That ever I was born to set things right.
MACBIRD: I don't believe you understand the job.
I wouldn't say you're asked to set things right.
I think you get the point. (II, 2, 48)

The attainment and retention of power are unmasked as a dirty business and the head of state is taunted.

Increasing escalation in Vietnam exposed Johnson to growing criticism following his clear electoral victory of 1964. His mismanagement of foreign policy resulting in the stepping up of the war, superimposed itself upon his domestic achievements of the years 1964 and 1965 in the context of his continuation of Kennedy's course of renewal with regard to civil rights, the combating of poverty, urban renewal, health care, environmental protection and the educational system. When after 1967, due to the costs of the war, less funding was available for reform measures and the American public reacted with shock and shame at the daily, televised images of brutality and alienation in South-East Asia, protest movements became radicalized and the wrath of the anti-war demonstrators united with the embitterment of the civil rights movement to form an explosive mixture. The political-societal consensus was lost. The country thus found itself in a profound crisis, "a canker of rage and frustration was eating away at America."[206] Serious unrest with violent conflicts and burning cities was the consequence encapsulated by "the terrible violence and chaos of the late sixties."[207] Frustration and rage was particularly aimed at the representative of the system, President Johnson. "How is it possible?" he asked, "after all we've accomplished? How could it be?"[208] He became a tragic figure, though not in the sense intended by Garson. Within the Democratic Party, Robert Kennedy and Eugene McCarthy distinguished themselves with an anti-war platform as strong competitors for the presidential elections of 1968.

MacBird! originated from within this context, first as a script for a teach-in against the war at the University of California at Berkeley, before being expanded into a play:

> Garson's play seems true to much of the protest movement of the sixties, to an anger propelled in large part by the frustration at finding no established authority that seemed capable of rescuing the country from the apparent abyss of Vietnam and racial strife.[209]

The piece is a marker for societal and cultural disintegration following Kennedy's death. The author attempts not only to win her public as allies against the head of government, but also, in the course of a radical rejection of the system, to distance it from the entire political class[210] and in fact to subversively undermine the body politic as a whole. It seems questionable, though, whether this subliminal invective against the entire political establishment is not in fact dominated by the far clearer, more emphatic anti-Johnson impact. Garson's recasts of Shakespeare's witches as Student Demonstrator, Negro and Old Leftist agitate against MacBird's "Smooth Society", the literary correlate to Johnson's Great Society. They symbolically set it on fire by projecting flames into the audience as the representative of society, with the incantatory formula "burn baby burn" (III, 4, 162). The cauldron, around which the witches gather, the "melting pot", is derived from the traditional, self-image of America, but reveals the nation to be ailing, internally torn and demoralized by violence, as exemplified by the plight of the African American minority:

> Club and gas and whip and gun,
> Niggers strung up just for fun.
> Round the cauldron chant and sing,
> Arson, rape and rioting.
> Bombed-out church and burning cross
> In the boiling cauldron toss.
> Black men beat and burnt and shot,
> Bake within our melting pot. (III, 2, 16-23)

While the horrors of Vietnam are also invoked:

> Sizzling skin of napalmed child,
> Roasted eyeballs, sweet and mild.

Now we add a fiery chunk
From a burning Buddhist monk.
Flaming field and blazing hut,
Infant fingers cooked and cut,
Young man's heart and old man's gut,
Groin and gall and gore of gook
In our cauldron churn and cook. (III, 2, 28-36)

Shakespeare's text already contains the aspect of disintegration as in *Macbeth*, various forms of dissolution and unnatural phenomena occur following the murder of the legitimate ruler, an act which violates the order of being according the correspondences between the degrees in the Elizabethan world picture. The disruption of the system is only overcome with the restoration of order through the removal of the disruptive factor, Macbeth himself, the guilty party. *MacBird!* transfers these notions of disorder and chaos to the time after Kennedy's assassination.

In Garson's drama, the destabilization of society includes striving against its norms and conventions of taste. Camp elements are found in the resulting challenge to the *haut gout* sensibilities of the addressees, in connection with irony, exaggeration, and theatrics. The underlying aesthetic of this mode of expression is a notoriously vague concept: "Anyone who has ever sent a tacky postcard to a friend knowing that they would 'get it,'" writes Gareth Cook, "understands camp, but a more precise definition is hard to come by."[211] In her approach to the phenomenon, Susan Sontag views various cultural artifacts, like Shakespeare's *Titus Andronicus*, texts by Alexander Pope and Horace Walpole, as well as Oscar Wilde, operas of Richard Strauss, the ballet *Swan Lake*, the film *The Maltese Falcon* and Tiffany lamps as camp.[212] She emphasizes that "the whole point of Camp is to dethrone the serious. Camp is playful, anti-serious. [...] One can be serious about the frivolous, frivolous about the serious."[213] Its motivations originate from the feeling that conventional possibilities for moving beyond seriousness – as *MacBird!* attempts in its gleefully subversive satire – are inadequate.[214] Camp therefore positions itself with ironizing irritations and inversions of existing standards in opposition to the striving for an aesthetic calibration of the collective consciousness, and thus undermines an assessment by the challenged mainstream culture right from the start. This also includes matters of taste. To this extent, the tastelessness of the play is deliberate. In the paradox "it's good because it's awful," Sontag correspondingly sees "the ultimate Camp statement."[215]

Wendy MacLeod appears to be conscious of the potential camp effect of her play when she immediately emphasizes the following in the advance "Author's Notes" to *The House of Yes*: "It is a great mistake to imagine the play is 'camp' because the characters pretend to be Jack and Jackie Kennedy."[216]

The main characters, Jackie-O and her twin brother Marty, have developed the ritual of reenacting the assassination with assigned roles and blank ammunition because the anniversary of Kennedy's death is of special importance to them:

MARTY. Do you still remember that day?
JACKIE-O. The day of the party?
MARTY. The day he was shot.
JACKIE-O. The radio was on, the TV was on.
MARTY. Mama was crying and Daddy was crying.
JACKIE-O. And Daddy was leaving.
MARTY. Finally leaving.
JACKIE-O. She covered him with her body. She tried to keep him there.
MARTY. She tried to keep his head on, but it was falling off.
JACKIE-O. You be him and I'll be her.
MARTY. I'm him?
JACKIE-O. And I'm her. (44-5)

Jackie-O points the gun at him and shoots. He falls. In slow motion they reenact the moments after Kennedy was assassinated. Jackie-O cradles Marty's head in her lap. Then she straddles him. Marty sits up as Jackie-O arches her back and moves in for a kiss.

The murder of the President and the loss of the father are brought together in an analogy, emphasized by the syntactic equivalency of the parallelisms and the references of the first names of the figures. The collectively and individually traumatizing blend together and undermine identity at both levels.

The recurring reenactment of the crime in the form of the assassination game can be seen as both a symptom of trauma and as part of the working through process.[217] Considering the symbolic place of Kennedy in the collective memory as the embodiment of an idealized American self-perception and self-assurance, the depth of the national trauma is conveyed, and the sustained and enduring fictionalization is explained. It does not help to forget the traumatizing memory, so instead one must overcome its dissociation and gain control over its content. As such the handling of the historical circumstances of the assassination serves the process of reconstruction of the national identity damaged by these events. "*The House of Yes* contribute[s] significantly to the process of working through that history,"[218] Bechtel observes and states:

> In the wake of our latest traumas, 9/11 and the most recent Iraq War [...] collective identity seems to have slipped even further out of our collective control. To regain both we must interrogate their traumatic loss, and repeat that trauma consciously and self-critically. This process can only be accomplished, however, if we first recognize the site of trauma, which is precisely the place where history returns. As a repetition that critiques the very act of repetition, *The House of Yes* returns history to us but strips it of its mask, showing us that the face beneath is our own.[219]

At the individual level, this coping process involves the dealings of the twins with their problematic past for the restoration of their damaged identities. This intensifies during a family weekend approximately twenty years after Kennedy's murder.

Marty returns home from New York for Thanksgiving to his mother, his twin sister, Jackie-O, and his younger brother, Anthony. The Pascals are neighbors of the Kennedys in the affluent Washington suburb of MacLean, Virginia. Jackie-O identifies with Jackie Kennedy, imitating her style and clothing. She often wears the pink Chanel suit from the day of the assassination. The question of whether the father abandoned the family on the day of Kennedy's death or was killed by his wife and buried in the backyard remains open.

Upon Marty's arrival, Anthony has just dropped out of Princeton and his sister has been out of a mental institution for several months. To the surprise of the family, Marty brings his fiancé, Lesly, with him to introduce her to his family, and thereby ruins the reunion. They arrive during a hurricane. Jackie-O, who has always wanted to have her brother to herself, initially reacts hysterically and then does everything in her power to keep Marty at home and have Lesly return to New York without him. For the sake of her daughter, Mrs. Pascal pursues the same goal. Jackie-O talks Anthony into sleeping with Lesly, which provides Mrs. Pascal with the reason to ask the fiancé to leave. However, when Marty decides to flee back to New York with Lesly to escape the dysfunctional family, his sister demands that they play the assassination game of the siblings one last time in the eye of the hurricane passing over them. In doing so she replaces the blanks with real ammunition and shoots her twin brother.

In the conflict between Jackie-O and Lesly, Marty decides in favor of his fiancé, because, in her contrast to the Pascals, Lesly is also the representative and voice of the normality he is striving for, which becomes clear when, among other things, she comprehensibly gets to the heart of things especially with regard to his sister:

> JACKIE-O. And if a certain person can't get the thing her heart is set on, a certain person goes insane. (*To Lesly, suddenly matter-of-fact.*) I suppose you think I'm going insane just to be fashionable.
> LESLY. I don't think you're insane.
> JACKIE-O. You don't think I'm insane?
> LESLY. No.
> JACKIE-O. You don't think I'm just an eensy-weensy bit insane?
> LESLY. I don't think you're insane. I think you're spoiled. (28)

Lesly comments as follows on Jackie-O living out her Jackie Kennedy fixation in the assassination suit with its artificial blood stains: "Look at yourself, look at your clothes, you're making fun of a woman who lost her husband, a man *died*, a man was *murdered*, a man who did something for other people …" (57).

Marty, in an anagnorisis, recognizes that he must leave behind the out-of-touch-with reality life with his twin sister and the rest of the family and return to New York. He declares: "I am tired of being above everything! I want to be a human being!" (43) In the attempt to restore his identity, he orients himself to normality and reality, while Jackie-O, in her imitation of Jackie Kennedy, has become caught in an illusion that includes her brother and outside of which she does not believe she will be able to exist. While she remains obsessively fixated on the past, he looks to the future (which, however, he will unfortunately not be able to realize).

The tragic events of Dallas lead to an assassination play within the play, which in turn leads back to tragedy. This circularity suggests inescapability, which is also reflected in the fact of being trapped in the house and in the problematic relationships due to the weather. The assassination becomes the matrix for tragedy and any usurpation by the comical does not last. The piece therefore develops into a hybrid tragicomedy with a fateful finale.

Yet it begins in the tradition of the screwball comedy following the pattern of the turbulent, esprit-charged comedies of the 1930s and early 1940s, with their disrespectful and pointed dialogue, and characterized by high paced and witty repartee (one of the most famous is Howard Hawks' *Bringing Up Baby* from 1938 with Katherine Hepburn and Cary Grant as a typically chaotic screw-ball couple). The subtext deals with sex – frivolous, but without being objectionable. The explicit is avoided, among other reasons because the Hays Code was in place in Hollywood from 1934; a codex of voluntary self-control for the acceptable representation of sexuality and violence. Following its abolition in 1967, greater liberality has prevailed, benefitting the high spirited frivolity of the genre, which includes more recently, among others, *Sex and the City*. This is also the case in *The House of Yes*.

This type of comedy is also borne by the effect of the ironic clash of opposites: rich and poor, educated and uneducated, appearance and being, playfulness and seriousness, illusion and reality, normal and overwrought, and especially, for the sake of the sex/ gender theme in the foreground, male and female. MacLeod's addition of the contrast between the comic and the tragic intensifies the latter and bursts the genre at the end of the piece. The consistent playing with the concepts of taste of the audience in connection with scurrility in the transition to pathology, as well as irony and theatrics, raises an impression, although not intended, of camp.

The manner of dealing with sexuality typical of the screwball comedy can also be read as an indicator of societal conditions. Like Barbara Garson, Wendy MacLeod takes recourse to the theater of the Stuart Period under James I and describes her drama in the subtitle as "A Suburban Jacobean Play" (9). One of its core features is that it "interrogates cultural ideals by scrutinizing sexual conduct."[220] An instance explaining this is offered by the infamous bisexual excesses at court well-known at the time, in the face of which questions of sexual morality were taken up critically and the social order with its prerogatives of the privileged placed in question. Both approaches are adopted in *The House of Yes* in its conception of itself as a Jacobean play. Inequalities and permissiveness are brought onto the stage and their co-responsibility for the murders insinuated.

The questioning of the social fabric, as in Jacobean Drama, is primarily accomplished through the constellation of characters. In a contrasting relationship to the Pascals, as representatives of the wealthy, who cultivate their elevated lifestyle with a weakness for European wines in a worldly ambience in affluent McLean, is Lesly, who comes from an unemployed family in structurally weak Pennsylvania, in which, for reasons of financial want, they mainly ate pancakes, and there wasn't enough money to take part in a school excursion. Jackie-O looks down her nose at her. She urges her siblings in a pseudo-sardonic fashion not to be "déclassé" (31) or "bourgeois" (32), not like "tiny people with tiny lives" (51), and treats "that Lesly-girl" (43), as she calls her, with habitual and calculated arrogance and a sharp tongue, not least with the intention to expose her in front of Marty:

JACKIE-O. Pancakes. Pancakes, Marty. And how did you pull yourself out? Out of poverty I mean.
LESLY. I left Pennsylvania.
JACKIE-O. That was a step in the right direction. Clearly. (*Lesly looks at the paintings hung on the wall.*) Do they have paintings in Pennsylvania?
MARTY. Jackie.
JACKIE-O. Well Marty I've never been to Pennsylvania, I've never even *met* anybody who's been to Pennsylvania, much less been *from* Pennsylvania, Pennsylvania is just this state that gets in your way when you have to go someplace else! (27)

The theme of social stratification is also the subject of the following passage of dialogue concerning Lesly's job as a waitress:

JACKIE-O. There is something I've been meaning to ask you. There's this thing I've heard and if I thought for one second it were true I would probably kill myself. Does your fiancée work in a donut shop?
MARTY. A Donut King. Actually.
JACKIE-O. A Donut King. So is she like the Queen? Are we entertaining royalty?
MARTY. She would be like a donut lady-in-waiting.
JACKIE-O. So she's sort of a marginal donut figure?
MARTY. In all fairness she is a minor and not a major donut figure. Because it's a chain you see, and there are women just like her all over the city.
JACKIE-O. My point exactly. (42)

The permissiveness thematized in the drama is the result of the trauma of losing the father/President, and is part of the dysfunctionality arising from it. Longing reminiscences of the time before November 22, 1963 suggest this again and again. The indulgent mother appears to be unable to handle the situation and takes refuge in a duel value system, which she represents with austere composure. For the outside world, the elevated atmosphere is upheld in keeping with the noble facade. Internally, out of concern for her sick daughter, she facilitates her egocentrism, just as she fails altogether to set boundaries and, in keeping with a broadly based policy of *laissez-faire*, allows her home to become a "house of yes". "The play," the author emphasizes, "is about people that have never been said no to" (5). The uncontrolled weather outside reflects the absence of order inside, including the internal turmoil of the main figures.

The collective "we" in a wall graffito cited by MacLeod, "we are living in a house of yes" (5), directs the focus in a generalizing way to society. Repeated references to the Kennedys being different make them the positive counterpart. This is given substance by Kennedy's rejection of a *laissez-faire* policy (like that of Coolidge) in favor of interventionist action. As a consequence, MacLeod does not handle contention and permissiveness conservatively, although she allows a maximum of liberality and *laissez-faire* to end in disaster.

Just like the individual I-identities prove to be not reconstituted at the end of the play and of the assassination game, the national we-identity sickens with the continuing effects of the assassination: "Just as Marty Pascal sought to reclaim his identity from the grip of traumatic possession America needs to work through its 'Kennedy trauma' as part of its own reclamation project."[221] *The House of Yes* is part and proof of this process. Numerous performances and the acclaim shown for the film version of Mark Waters with Parker Posey (Jackie-O) and Tori Spelling (Lesly) speak for its topicality, enduring decades after the murder of the President – including an award at the 1997 Sundance Film Festival.

In poetry the primary focus is also on Kennedy's death and forms the second part of a development of the national discourse on identity and commemoration with Robert Frost's poem "The Gift Outright" contributing to the first. He subjects this to revision though during his recitation at Kennedy's inauguration.

The text, published for the first time in 1942, provides a critical meditation on America's past and the construction of (cultural) identity affiliated with it. This did not take place in the colonial period of the 17th and 18th centuries, according to the speaker, because, while the colonists may have appropriated the country in the north and the south, they themselves still belonged to England as the colonial power:

> The land was ours before we were the land's.
> She was our land more than a hundred years
> Before we were her people. She was ours
> In Massachusetts, in Virginia.

But we were England's, still colonials,
Possessing what we still were unpossessed by,
Possessed by what we now no more possessed.[222]

With the frontier advancing westward in the 19th century, according to Turner, the main factor in the Americanization of the country and its inhabitants, only vague progress ("the land vaguely realizing westward") was made – a view not qualified with manifest destiny rhetoric. The new inhabitants completely ("outright") committed themselves to the country, but the role of literature and art as shapers of national identity had not yet found adequate recognition and consideration.

The text's attempt at memorializing and shaping the past of a nation lacking an as yet complete collective consciousness is seen as compensation for this absence: "'The Gift Outright' expresses the formlessness of the American experience as well as the poet's desire for form."[223]

The tension between this striving for form and its incompleteness is reflected in the poem's composition. With the opposition of the continuously binding blankverse preferred by Frost and applied repeatedly in the text ("I do not write free verse; I write in blankverse") [224] and iambic tetrameter and hexameter, a uniform and complete formation with unrhymed iambic pentameter does not come about. The structure, with a tendency toward free verse, is kept open. Varying lengths of lines and the dispensing with a stanzaic breakdown point in the same direction. The breaking through of the conventionalized blankverse brought over from the English mother country toward free verse can be read as a Whitmanesque expression of stylistic independence from the poetological prescriptions of the Old World.[225]

An aesthetic of becoming instead of being, of the dynamic instead of the static, of the process-oriented instead of the complete manifests itself in the suspension of regularity combined with the thematic emphasis on imperfection (of the formation of identity and consciousness). It harmonizes with the indistinct, still subjunctively expressed outlook at the end:

Such as we were we gave ourselves outright
(The deed of gift was many deeds of war)
To the land vaguely realizing westward,
But still unstoried, artless, unenhanced,
Such as she was, such as she would become.

In this original version of the poem, the perspective is toward the past and, although only vaguely, forward into the future, but hardly synchronously to the present. This latter aspect is first incorporated in the dedication poem for Kennedy's inauguration, as part of which the author presented "The Gift Outright" in this new situation in a revised version.

With Robert Frost a representative of the realm of literature is heard at the inauguration of a new president for the first time on January 20, 1961. In his prepared text, the poet initially pays tribute to the role now admitted to the arts in public life:

Summoning artists to participate
In the August occasions of the state
Seems something artists ought to celebrate.
Today is for my cause a day of days.
And his be poetry's old-fashioned praise
Who was the first to think of such a thing.
This verse that in acknowledgement I bring
Goes back to the beginning of the end
Of what had been for centuries the trend;
A turning point in modern history.[226]

He welcomes his participation in the inauguration in the present as this "point of 'enhancement'",[227] the absence of which he had lamented in the past in "The Gift Outright". "Frost finds here the recognition, the momentary fulfillment of his dream of the poet as civilizing agent."[228] Following these introductory verses, his manuscript addresses the optimistic idea that, with Kennedy in the White House, a "golden age" will commence, comparable with the *Saeculum Augustum,* the period of rule of Gaius Octavius Augustus, vaunted for its internal stability, prosperity, security, and the blossoming of literature and art (including Horace, Ovid, and Virgil):

It makes the prophet in us all presage
The glory of a next Augustan age
Of a power leading from its strength and pride,
Of young ambition eager to be tried,
Firm in our free beliefs without dismay,
In any game the nations want to play.
A golden age of poetry and power
Of which this noonday's the beginning hour.[229]

Blinded by the sun and snow on the cold winter's day of the inauguration ceremony, the 86-year old is unable to read off these lines. He nonetheless expresses his belief in a positive future beginning with the new President, in that he recites "The Gift Outright" from memory and, in doing so, dispenses with the subjunctive for the foresight in the last verse on this occasion: "[...] such as she *will* become [italics mine]."[230]

Considering the breadth of the positive echo from authors such as W.H. Auden, Ernest Hemingway, Archibald MacLeish, Norman Mailer John Steinbeck, and E.B. White with reference to Kennedy's assumption of office,[231] this affirmation can claim a certain representativeness and is not only grounded in the epideictics of the occasion.

Against this background, the scope, quality and tenor of the literary reactions to his death, which also cannot be overlooked in poetry, are hardly surprising. John Berryman's "Formal Elegy" places the start of the disintegration after Kennedy's death in a direct relationship with the assassination and demonstrates how this event is neither understood nor got to grips with, how it appears devoid of sense and meaning and thus leaves an impression of disorientation and unreality. It remains inaccessible to ordering, controlling, and rational access.

The term "scene of disorder"[232] used by the lyrical I is revealing. There is no structure borne by a rhyme scheme, no discernable metric pattern or strophic form. The ten units each encompass between two and twenty lines of various lengths, and offer a non-linear sequence of scattered scraps of perception, in some cases adopted from television, of Kennedy, Oswald, Dallas, death and Arlington. They flow into one another, which is underlined by the run-on lines which force the reader to continue without interruptions or time to consider them, while, caesuras rupture the lines. Verses like "overwhelmed-un, live" (47) are devoid of both a regular morphological and a syntactic structure. The absence of order is further emphasized by the contrasting effect with the announcement of a "formal elegy" in the title. "Yes. it looks like a wilderness" (44), the speaker states. The sequence of medial stimuli appears to him as a "black foam" (45), which reinforces the unreality of the experience: "not wholly real" (45). Paralyzed, "stunned", and "constrained to weep" (45), the self stares at the TV images without achieving a coherent impression of reality. Just as unreal is the following fancy: "I do all-wish the bullets swim astray/ sent to the President" (46).

The attempt of this elegy to overcome confusion and chaos and to find access to meaning or a comforting perspective fails. It is a keening that lends language to the inability to mentally grasp the situation, to comprehend it, in order to be able to deal with it appropriately. A feeling of helplessness, of being overwhelmed, of powerlessness and unreality, without a meaningful interpretation is revealed, which suggests a posttraumatic condition. Through the verbalization of such a state this confessional poetry seeks to achieve a self-therapeutic improvement of the cognitive processes of working through the event, and through that process find a means of coping with it.

Carol Bergé also reproduces injury and confusion in her jazz poem "Pavane for the White Queen" with the "voices of broken bells", the paradox of the "sound of torn strings", and the oxymoron of a "silent scream". The masculine cadences in connection with the verbless stringing together of thought fragments thus convey a corresponding state of agitation:

> Not as the word death, but
> as confusion: memory of bells
> into voices of broken bells,

sound of torn strings: songs
into this silent scream.[233]

Similarly, the first lines of Allen Ginsberg's "Nov. 23, 1963: Alone" already point towards such a reaction, a disruption of the self-concept:

Alone
in that same self where I always was
with Kennedy throat brain bloodied in Texas[234]

"Alone" stands alone, as the only word of the first line, which clearly differentiates it from all other, longer verses, and focuses attention on the solitary adjective. A semantic opposition commencing from this point defines the subsequent structure of the poem, because the feeling of being abandoned addressed at the start stands in opposition to a long list of people and processes by which the speaker is surrounded in this situation. They are bundled together to form a massive, juxtaposed sense unit by a recurring, thirty-fold anaphora:

with Charlie muttering in his underwear strewn bedroom
with Neal running down the hall shouting about the racetrack
with Ann with her white boy's ass silent under the Cupid thigh
with Lucille talking to herself, feeding the pregnant cat Alice
with Anne [...][235]

This is intensified by the self being exposed to an uninterrupted flood of messages via telephone, TV and print media (primarily underground magazines). The apparent contradiction between the feeling of being alone and being surrounded by the numerous people and activities of a countercultural community underlines the fact that the subject does not find itself externally isolated, but rather "alone" and estranged within itself as a consequence of its identity being shaken by Kennedy's murder. Further symptoms are shock and confusion: "with myself confused shock-fingertips."[236] Here too, the speaker is distraught and overwhelmed. The various impressions are placed next to one another paratactically as fragments without transition; they are not subject to any kind of hierarchical order. The same applies to the syntax in expressions like: "with Kennedy throat brain bloodied in Texas." This mode of presentation communicates the experience of confusion in keeping with the anti-hierarchical stance characteristic of the beat poets and Ginsberg's "freedom of composition"[237]. It once more voices the feeling of the loss of a coherent reality described by DeLillo and others. The unreflected, immediate expression of such inner states serves the freedom of composition advocated by the poet, who seeks unpremeditated expressiveness, spontaneous and to be atuned to the natural and unhampered flow of breath, instead of one restricted by formal superimpositions. Influenced by the improvisations of jazz and the repetitive patterns of Far Eastern mantras, "Nov.23, 1963: Alone" realizes one of Ginsberg's declared goals, "full force of feeling [...] slowly developed and outwardly expressed in solitude"[238] on the occasion of Kennedy's death.

Another voice of the counterculture, the speaker in Lou Reed's "The Day John Kennedy Died", likewise expresses incomprehension:

> I dreamed that there was a point in life and to the human race
> I dreamed that I could somehow comprehend that someone
> Shot him in the face.[239]

The anaphora, "I dreamed," underlines that understanding is only possible in the world of imagination, but not in reality. Nonetheless this text suggests a transition to poetry which expresses the inner state of confusion, but no longer as something static. Therefore the preöccupation with the trauma is less clearly recognizable, but instead gives way to a coping strategy. Self-commitment to the values represented by the mourned for person is shown in Reed's text to be an aspect of "normal" grieving with the prospect of eventually accepting or bearing the loss experienced. In contrast to the previous poems, here a high degree of regularity and order is established through a clear division into stanzas, many of them identical in structure, with recurrent anaphoras, with parallelisms and rhymes, which indicates that the lyrical is gaining control:

> I dreamed I was the president of these United States
> I dreamed I replaced ignorance, stupidity and hate
> I dreamed the perfect union and a perfect law, undenied
> And most of all I dreamed I forgot the day John Kennedy died
>
> I dreamed that I could do the job that others hadn't done
> I dreamed that I was uncorrupt and fair to everyone
> I dreamed I wasn't gross or base, a criminal on the take
> And most of all I dreamed I forgot the day John Kennedy died.

W.H. Auden's "Elegy for J.F.K.", which was set to music in 1964 by Igor Stravinsky for the piece of music of the same name to commemorate Kennedy, also develops beyond the problem of incomprehensibility. At the beginning:

> Why *then*? Why *there*?
> Why *thus*, we cry, did he die?[240]

However, this is then followed by the appeal to the collective obligation to pursue Kennedy's goals in the second and third haiku-like stanzas. In that they are integrated into a meaningful context, which provides memory with a sense of orientation instead of giving it over to confusion, through this both meditative and dynamic structure, a possibility for dealing with the event is offered in this elegy. The quiet tone and the regular style deepen the impression of a turnaround in the direction of consolation as an element of coping. In keeping with Auden's basic understanding of a poem as a rite ("a poem is a rite; hence its formal and ritualistic character")[241], "Elegy for J.F.K" thus assumes the role of a comforting, traditional lament that provides sense:

What he was, he was:
What he is fated to become
Depends on us.

Remembering his death.
How we choose to live
Will decide its meaning.

Richard Holler's "Abraham, Martin and John" is subject to a comparable approach. The interpretations of Harry Belafonte, Bon Jovi, Dion, Bob Dylan, Emmylou Harris and Whitney Houston, as well as a position at the top of the charts and various music video versions, have seen it exert considerable influence on the collective memory. Harris places the lyrics in relation to "It's a Hard Life Wherever You Go" by Nancy Griffith, a wrathful indictment of hate, prejudice, and the withholding of a perspective for the following generation:

A dairy line in Chicago
The man in front of me
Is calling black people trash to his children
He's the only trash here I see.

And I'm thinking this man wears a white hood
In the night when his children should sleep
But they slip to their window and see him
And think that white hoods are all they need.[242]

This negative image, in which the resigned self presents itself as the "backseat driver from America", "not at the wheel of control", is opposed in the riposte by Abraham Lincoln, Martin Luther King, John and Robert Kennedy as "old friends" of the underprivileged, as symbols of liberation and of social change, as positive points of orientation:

Anybody here seen my old friend Abraham?
Can you tell me where he's gone?
He freed a lotta people but it seems the good they die young.
You know I just looked around and he's gone.

Anybody here seen my old friend John?
Can you tell me where he's gone?
He freed a lotta people but it seems the good they die young.
I just looked around and he's gone.[243]

Here too, the lament is followed by the appeal:

Didn't you love the things that they stood for?
Didn't they try to find some good for you and me?

Notes

1 Michael O'Brien, *John F. Kennedy: A Biography*, New York: Thomas Dunne, 2005, XVII.
2 "Kennedy Has Become America's Favorite President", *Newsweek*, November 28, 1983, 36.
3 O'Brien, XVII.
4 Lydia Saad, "JFK and Ronald Reagan Win Gallup Presidents Day Poll", Gallup News Service, February 18, 2008 <http://www.gallup.com/poll/104380/JFK-Ronald-Reagan-Win-Gallup-Presidents-Day-Poll.aspx > (March 6, 2009).
5 Robert Dallek, *An Unfinished Life: John F. Kennedy, 1917-1963,* New York: Little, Brown & Co., 2003, 700.
6 C-Span 2009, Historians Presidential Leadership Survey < http://www.c-span.org/Presidential Survey/Overall-Ranking.aspx> (March 15, 2010).
7 Thomas Brown, *JFK: History of an Image*, Bloomington: Indiana University Press, 1988, 16.
8 Dallek, 574.
9 Ted Sorensen, *Counselor: A Life at the Edge of History*, New York: HarperCollins, 2008, 340.
10 July 2, 2007, cover.
11 David Talbot, "Warrior for Peace", July 2, 2007, 44.
12 Irving Bernstein, *Promises Kept: John F. Kennedy's New Frontier*, New York, Oxford: Oxford University Press, 1991, 7.
13 Vii.
14 Sorensen, 521.
15 Arthur Schlesinger, *A Thousand Days: John F. Kennedy in the White House*, Greenwich, Conn.: Fawcett, 1965, 939.
16 Nigel Hamilton, *Life and Death of an American President, Vol I: Reckless Youth*, London: Century, 1992, 81.
17 Xxiv.
18 John Hellmann, *The Kennedy Obsession: The American Myth of JFK*, New York: Columbia University Press, 1997, 29.
19 *The Kennedy Imprisonment: A Meditation on Power,* New York: Pocket, 1981, 152.
20 "Kennedy: Myth and History", *John F. Kennedy: Person, Policy, Presidency*, ed. J. Richard Snyder, Wilmington, Del.: SR, 1988, 32.
21 Hellmann, ix.
22 O'Brien's term, XVI.
23 Wills, 152.
24 John Kifner, "The Nation: Once More With Feeling: Recycling the Kennedys", *The New York Times*, November 16, 1997, 414.
25 Thomas Reeves, *A Question of Character: A Life of John F. Kennedy*, New York: The Free Press, 1991, 414.
26 Kifner, 4.
27 *Ib.*
28 Peter Charles Hoffer explains it as a psychological reaction to the feeling of loss:

> Having chided and pushed us out into the world, he then abandoned us by dying. He left us to finish the work, bereft (and no scholar, detractor, or defender can deny how

> bereft we felt), and alone [...] It seems to me, some scholars of my generation resent the unfulfilled promises of Kennedy's administration, and redirect that resentment against the man himself;

"Kennedy and the Regeneration of America", *John F. Kennedy: Person, Policy, Presidency*, 43.

29 Heather Nielsen, "Jack's Ghost: Reappearances of John F. Kennedy in the Work of Gore Vidal and Norman Mailer", *American Studies International*, 35:3, 1997, 23-41.

30 "An Assassination and Its Fictions", Hellmann, 145-179 iconographically devotes itself to a limited range of assassination fiction.

31 Aleida Assmann, *Einführung in die Kulturwissenschaft*, Berlin: Erich Schmidt, 2008, 191.

32 Barbie Zelizer, *Covering the Body: The Kennedy Assassination, the Media, and the Shaping of Collective Memory*, Chicago: University of Chicago Press, 1992, 4.

33 Astrid Erll, *Gedächtnisromane: Literatur über den Ersten Weltkrieg als Medium englischer und deutscher Erinnerungskulturen in den 1920iger Jahren*, Trier: Wissenschaftlicher Verlag Trier, 2003, 67.

34 Don DeLillo, *Libra*, London: Penguin, 1988, 392.

35 O'Brien, 900.

36 "Dallas Echoing Down the Decades", *The New York Times*, July 24, 1988 <http://www.ny-times.com/s/97/03/ 16/lifetimes/del-r-libra.html?> (November 19, 2010).

37 "PW Interviews: Don DeLillo", *Conversations With Don DeLillo*, ed. Thomas dePietro, Jackson: University Press of Mississippi, 2005, 50.

38 Anthony deCurtis, "'An Outsider In This Society': An Interview With Don DeLillo", *Conversations With Don DeLillo*, 58.

39 New York, London: Routledge, 1988, 20.

40 21.

41 "History, Biography, and Narrative in Don DeLillos's *Libra*-novel about Lee Harvey Oswald", *Twentieth Century Literature*, 43:1, Spring 1997, 109.

42 Jamie Stengle, "Kennedy sibling doubts that one shooter killed JFK", *The Palm Beach Post*, January 13, 2013, A 7.

43 "Onward and Upward with the Arts", June 24, 1967, 70.

44 Zelizer, 112.

45 *Report of the Select Committee on Assassinations: Findings and Recommendations*, Washington: Government Printing Office, 1979, 256.

46 261.

47 *Final Report of the Select Committee on Assassinations: Summary of Findings and Recommendations*, Washington. Government Printing Office, 1979, 3.

48 *Final Report of the Select Committee on Assassinations: Findings and Recommendations*, 261.

49 161.

50 Zelizer, 119.

51 London: Hodder & Stoughton.

52 Wilfried Huismann, *Rendevous mit dem Tod*, München: Pendo, 2006, 209-12.

53 *The Plot to Kill the President*, New York: Times, 1981.

54 Zelizer, 111.

55 Gerald Posner, *Case Closed: Lee Harvey Oswald and the Assassination of JFK*, New York: Random House, 1993, ix.

56 "Introduction", New York: Greenwood Press, 1988, xii.

57 December 8, 1983, 22.

58 London: Penguin, [[1]1971] 1989, 377.

59 *The Tokyo-Montana Express*, London: Pan, 1980, 43.

60 December 7, 1983.
61 *Postmodernism in the Fiction of Richard Brautigan*, Diss., Middle Tennessee State University, 1985, 164.
62 *Richard Brautigan. Pounding at the Gates of American Literature*, Heidelberg: Carl Winter, Universitätsverlag, 1986, 217; translation mine.
63 Washington, D.C., January 20, 1961, *Let the Word Go Forth: The Speaches, Statements, and Writings of John F. Kennedy*, ed. Theodore C. Sorensen, New york: Delacorte Press, 1988, 140.
64 Harmondsworth: Penguin, 1968, 325.
65 "Updike's American Comedies", *John Updike*, ed. Harold Bloom, Philadelphia: Chelsea House, 1986, Modern Critical Views, 57.
66 Tony Tanner, "A Compromised Environment", Bloom, 51.
67 53.
68 *One Day*, Lincoln: University of Nebraska Press, 1965, 31.
69 *Wright Morris Revisted*, New York: Twayne, 1998, 123.
70 "What Was It Like to be Oneself?" *The New York Times*, March 7, 1963, 32.
71 See William Manchester, *Controversy*, Arthur Schlesinger, *Robert Kennedy and His Times*, 818-23, and Gary Wills, *The Kennedy Imprisonment*, 109-15.
72 *The Death of a President*, New York, London: Harper & Row, 1967, 30.
73 "Documentary Narrative as Art: William Manchester and Truman Capote", *The Reporter as Artist: A Look At the New Journalism Controversy*, ed. Ronald Weber, New York: Hastings House 1974, 212.
74 New York, London: Bantam, [1958] 1972, 19.
75 18.
76 New York: Simon & Schuster, 2007, 279.
77 207-19.
78 "The newspaper as literature/ literature as leadership", *shake it for the world*, London: Allison & Busby, 1971, 357.
79 "'Literary Journalism' as an Epistemological Moving Object Within a Larger 'Quantum' Narrative", *Journal of Communication Inquiry* 1999, 23, 432.
80 William F. Buckley, *See You Later Alligator*, London: Arrow, 1985, 1.
81 "The Problems to Come: Kennedy's Solution to Problems May Prove Radical in Long Run", January 20, 1961, 1.
82 "Televised Address on Berlin Crisis", Washington, D.C., July 25, 1961, Sorensen, 1988, 262.
83 The Senate Foreign Relations Subcommittee on Latin America questioned Goodwin on August 31 and finally concluded that his meeting with Guevara was "informal".
84 Goodwin, *Remembering America: A Voice from the Sixties*, New York: Harper & Row, 1988, 203.
85 206-8.
86 O'Brien, *John F. Kennedy*, 680.
87 Richard Reeves, *President Kennedy: Profile of Power*, New York: Simon & Schuster, 1993, 347.
88 Robert S. Thomson, *The Missiles of October: The Declassified Story of John F. Kennedy and the Cuban Missile Crisis*. New York: Simon & Schuster, 1992, 165.
89 Tad Szulc,"Modernized Army Called Cuba's Aim", *The New York Times*, September 3, 1962, 2.
90 *The Kennedy Tapes: Inside the White House during the Cuban Missile Crisis*, ed. Ernest R. May and Philip D. Zelikow, Cambridge: The Belknap Press of Harvard University Press, 1997, 187-244.
91 Decades later it became known that about 90 such warheads were being made operational (Robert S. McNamara, *In Retrospect*, New York: Times, Random House, 1995, 341) – one of the pieces of information *ex post* which show that the world was in fact at the brink of nuclear war.

92 See Raymond L. Garthoff, "US Intelligence and the Cuban Missile Crisis", *Intelligence and the Cuban Missile Crisis*, ed. James G. Blight, David A. Welsh, London: Frank Cass, 1998, 23.
93 Goodwin, 199.
94 Stefan Kanfer, "Fly on the Wall: *See You Later Alligator*", *Time*, February 4, 1985, 74.
95 Bernd Lenz, *Factifiction: Agentenspiele wie in der Realität – Wirklichkeitsanspruch und Wirklichkeitsgehalt des Agentenromans*, Heidelberg: Carl Winter, Universitätsverlag, 1987, 62.
96 *Miles Gone by*, Washington, D.C.: Regnery, 2004, 345-6; *The Blackford Oakes Reader*, New York: toExcel, 1995, xv-xvi; *The Right Word*, New York: Harcort Brace & Co., 1996, 242-4.
97 2004, 346.
98 344.
99 *Ib.*
100 Buckley, *The Right Word,* 337-341, Mailer, *The Presidential Papers*, Frogmore: Panther, [[1]1964] 1977, 175-189.
101 "The Company They Keep", *The New York Times Review*, September 29, 1991, 26.
102 David Rampton, "Plexed Artistry. The Formal Case for *Harlot's Ghost*", *Journal of Modern Literature*, 30:1, 2006, 50.
103 New York: Plume , 1968.
104 219.
105 New York: Random House, 1991, 1132.
106 Wilfried Sheed, "Armageddon Now?" *The New York Review of Books*, December 5, 1991 <http://nys.com/article/articles-preview> (June 20, 2010).
107 London: Panther, 1972, 9.
108 London: Panther, [[1]1964] 1977, 11.
109 35.
110 34.
111 Anton Myrer, *The Last Convertible*, New York: Berkley, 1979, 330.
112 *Der historische Roman in England und Amerika*, Darmstadt: Wissenschaftliche Buchgesellschaft, 1981, 53; translation mine.
113 37; translation mine.
114 *"Johnny, We Hardly Knew Ye": Memories of John Fitzgerald Kennedy*, New York: Kangaroo, 1972, 77.
115 See also the correspondences between the historiographic and literary versions in *Johnny, We Hardly Knew Ye"*, 77 and *The Last Convertible*, 331.
116 Schabert's term, 71.
117 Herbert Mitgang, "Behind the Bestsellers: Anton Myrer", *The New York Times Book Review*, May 28, 1978, 6.
118 *The Last Convertible*, cover.
119 O'Donnell *et al.*, 80.
120 *Ib.*
121 *Ib.*
122 O'Brien, 200.
123 *John F. Kennedy and a New Generation*, Boston: Little, Brown & Company, 1988, 22.
124 John Bodnar, *The Transplanted: A History of Immigrants in Urban America*, Bloomington: Indiana University Press, 1985, 203.
125 Edward M. Kennedy, *True Compass*, [London]: Little, Brown, 2009, 46.
126 "Intimations of Mortality", *Time*, February 10, 1967 <http:/time.com/time/magazine/article/0.9171.840865-2.00html>(July 29, 2010).

127 *Ib.*
128 *The man who knew Kennedy*, [New York]: Dial Press, 1967, 3
129 "Intimations of Mortality".
130 Stephen Graubard, *The Presidents: The Transformation of the American Presidency from Theodore Roosevelt to George W. Bush*, New York, London: Penguin, 2004, 222.
131 *Unspeakable Practices, Unnatural Acts,* New York: Farrar, Straus & Giroux, 1968, 37.
132 Walter Jackson Hicks, *An Essay on Recent American Fiction,* Chapel Hill: University of North Carolina, Press, 1974, 11-12.
133 "Donald Barthelmes *fictions*: Fragmente aus Wörtern mit Würmern", *American Studies* 19, 1974, 129; translation mine.
134 Jack Hicks, *In the Singer's Temple*, Chapel Hill: University of North Carolina Press, 1981, 51.
135 *Arthur Schlesinger, Robert Kennedy and His Times,* New York: Ballantines, 1978, 877.
136 878.
137 877.
138 Robert Rauschenberg: Im Gespräch mit Barbara Rose, Cologne: Kiepenheuer & Witsch, 1989, 116; translation mine.
139 *The New York Times Review*, September 3, 1989, 9.
140 *The Shape of the Art in the Short Stories of Donald Barthelme*, Baton Rouge: Louisiana State University Press, 1985, 163.
141 Lois Gordon, *Donald Barthelme*, Boston: Twayne, 1981, 92.
142 97.
143 Stengel, 171
144 93.
145 Winfried Fluck, *Inszenierte Wirklichkeit: Der amerikanische Realismus, 1865-1890*, Munich: Fink, 1992, 12.
146 *Ib.*
147 Brown, 21.
148 20.
149 < http://religiousfreedom.lib.virginia.edusacred/charity.html> (October 13, 2008).
150 Seymour Martin Lipset, *American Exceptionalism: A Double-Edged Sword*, New York: Norton, 1996, 18.
151 John Kane, "American Values or Human Rights? U.S. Foreign Policy and the Fractured Myth of Virtuous Power", *Presidential Studies Quarterly*, 33: 4, December 2003, 778.
152 779-80.
153 *Diplomacy*, New York: Simon & Schuster, 1994, 809.
154 Kane, 780-81.
155 Brown, 107.
156 David Burner, *John F. Kennedy and a New Generation*, Boston, London: Little, Brown & Co., 169.
157 22.
158 Th. Reeves, 87.
159 *The Making of the President 1960,* New York: Mentor, 1961, 179.
160 Louis Harris, *The Anguish of Change*, New York: Norton, 1973, 200.
161 *Kennedy and the Promise of the Sixties*, Cambridge: Cambridge University Press, 2002, 227.
162 "Opening Statement, First Televised Presidential Candidates Debate", Chicago, Ill., September 26, 1960, Sorensen 1988, 105.
163 "Nomination Acceptance Speech", July 25, 98.
164 102.

165 101.

166 *Ib.*

167 *Ib.*

168 Unsettled by the speech, Ronald Reagan wrote to Kennedy's opponent, Richard Nixon: "Under the tousled boyish hair cut it is still old Karl Marx – first launched a century ago;" Edmund Morris, *Dutch: A Memoir of Ronald Reagan*, New York: Random House, 1999, 316.

169 Rorabaugh, xviii.

170 Xvii.

171 Xix.

172 Xvii.

173 A film version with Vanessa Redgrave and Richard Harris followed in 1967.

174 "Finale Ultimo", *Camelot*, CD: Motion Picture Soundtrack, Warner Brothers Records [n. d.].

175 O'Brien, XIII.

176 "The Legacy of JFK: Reflections on the President, the Man and the Myth", *Newsweek*, November 28, 1983, 37.

177 *Ib.*

178 "Camelot Revisited", *The New Yorker*, June 5, 1995, 33.

179 Th. Reeves, 4-5.

180 The indispositions referred to in the novels are not the only ones:

> To make matters worse, Kennedy also suffered from colitis, prostrate and urinary tract problems, allergies, high cholesterol, and occasional insomnia. He received Phenobarbital for sleeplessness, penicillin and other antibiotics for his urinary tract infections, and Stelazine for anxiety.

Nonetheless, Robert E. Gilbert emphasizes Kennedy's unlimited ability to govern:

> Although Kennedy suffered from a litany of medical conditions and was taking a myriad of medications, he was in no way a disabled president. In his almost three years in the White House, he missed only one day of work because of illness and his leadership was not impaired in any significant aspect by his physical indispositions.

"*The Contemporary Presidency*: The Twenty-Fifth Amendment: Recommendations and Deliberations of the Working Group on Presidential Disability", *Presidential Studies Quarterly*, 33:4, 2003, 886.

181 "The Union Justified the Means", *The New York Times Book Review*, June 3, 1984, 1.

182 O'Brien, 681.

183 November 28, 1983, 33.

184 "The Kennedy Legacy", *Newsweek*, November 28, 1983, 38.

185 "Recapturing the Past: Introduction", *Trauma: Explorations in Memory*, ed. Cathy Caruth, Baltimore, London: Johns Hopkins University Press, 1995, 153.

186 They emphasize the ideas of the French psychoanalyst Pierre Janet developed in *L'automatismé Psychologiqué* (1989) and *Les Medication Psychologiques* (1919-25); "The Intrusive Past: The Flexibility of Memory and the Engraving of Trauma", Caruth 160.

187 Roger Bechtel, *Past Performance: American Theater and the Historical Imagination*, Lewisburg: Bucknell University Press, 2007, 91.

188 93.

189 92.

190 71.

191 Van der Hart, van der Kolk, 176.

192 Caruth, 153.

193 *Let the Word Go Forth*, 290.
194 Westport, Conn.: Praeger, 1996, 150.
195 Houndmills, London: Macmillan Press, 1996, 239.
196 392.
197 Dallek, 709.
198 "Kennedy and a New Generation", *John F. Kennedy: Person, Policy, Presidency*, ed. J. Richard Snyder, Wilmington, Del.: SR, 1988, 22.
199 *Profiles in Courage*, New York: Harper, [^{1}1955] 2003, 217.
200 "Vergnügen mit Hexen", *Der Spiegel*, 10, February 27, 1967, 122.
201 *Ib.*
202 John H. Houchin, *Censorship of the American Theatre in the Twentieth Century*, Cambridge, New York: Cambridge University Press, 2003, 193.
203 *Ib.*
204 *MacBird!*, Berkeley: Grassy Knoll Press, 1966, 5.
205 Bechtel, 96.
206 Morris Dickstein, *Gates of Eden: American Culture in the Sixties*, New York: Basic, 1977, 257.
207 Rorabaugh, Xvii.
208 E. Kennedy, 246.
209 Thomas Blackburn, "*MacBird!* and *Macbeth*: Topicality and Imitation in Barbara Garson's Satirical Pastiche", *Macbeth and Its Afterlife*, ed. Peter Holland, Cambridge: Cambridge University Press, 2004, 143.
210 Norbert Platz refers to a corresponding characterization of Robert in *MacBird!*, who presumably occupies the place of Duncan's sons Malcolm and Donalbain, in "Barbara Garson, *MacBird!*", *Anglo-Amerikanische Shakespeare-Bearbeitungen des 20. Jahrhunderts*, ed. Horst Prießnitz, Darmstadt: Wissenschaftliche Buchgesellschaft, 1980, 385-98.
211 "The dark side of camp – analysis of camp style and society", *Washington Monthly*, September 1995 < 2http://findarticles.com/p/articles/mi_m1316/is_n9_v27/17292791> (May 2, 2010).
212 "Notes on 'Camp'", *Against Interpretation and other Essays*, New York: Picador, [^{1}1961] 1966, 277-8.
213 288.
214 *Ib.*
215 292.
216 *The House of Yes*, New York: Dramatists Play Service, 1996, 5.
217 Bechtel, 99-100.
218 99.
219 100.
220 Albert H. Tricomi, *Reading Tudor-Stuart Texts Through Cultural Historicism*, Gainesville, Fl.: University Press of Florida, 1996, 108.
221 Bechtel, 98.
222 *Of Poetry and Power: Poems Occasioned by the Presidency and by the Death of John F. Kennedy*, ed. Erwin A. Glikes and Paul Schwaber, New York: Basic, 1964, 10.
223 Hamida Bosmaijan, "Robert Frost's 'The Gift Outright': Wish and Reality in History and Poetry", *American Quarterly*, 22:1, 1970, 101.
224 *Interviews with Robert Frost*, ed. Edward C. Lathem, Guildford, Conn.: Jeffrey Norton, 1997, 52.
225 See also his "Facing West From California's Shores", in which the offer of such emancipation is especially thematized as a literary contribution to the emergence of a national culture.
226 "For John F. Kennedy His Inauguration", Glikes and Schwaber, 7.

227 Harvey Shapiro, "The Story of a Poem", *New York Times Magazine*, January 15, 1961, 6.
228 Bosmaijan, 103.
229 Glikes and Schwaber, 7.
230 10.
231 Schlesinger 1965, 671-2.
232 Glikes and Schwaber, 47.
233 121.
234 *Collected Poems 1947-1997*, New York, London: Penguin, 2009, 341-2.
235 *Ib.*
236 *Ib.*
237 Allen Ginsberg, "When the Mode of the Music Changes, the Walls of the City Shake", *Deliberate Prose: Selected Essays 1952-1995 – Allen Ginsberg*, ed. Bill Morgan, New York: HarperCollins, 2000, 247.
238 "Reflections on the Mantra", Morgan, 149.
239 *The Blue Mask,* [CD] BMG Entertainment International, [[1]1982] 1999.
240 Glikes and Schwaber, 121.
241 *Making, Knowing, and Judging*, Oxford: Oxford University Press, 1957, 31.
242 Emmylou Harris and the Nash Ramblers, [CD] *At the Ryman*, Reprise, 1992.
243 *Ib.*

Bibliography

Auden, W.H. *Making, Knowing, and Judging*. Oxford: Oxford University Press, 1957.

–, "Elegy for J.F.K." In *Of Poetry and Power: Poems Occasioned by the Presidency and by the Death of John F. Kennedy*. Edited by Erwin A. Glikes and Paul Schwaber. New York: Basic, 1964. 121.

Assmann, Aleida. *Einführung in die Kulturwissenschaft*. Berlin: Erich Schmidt, 2008.

Barth, John. "Thinking Man's Minimalist: Honoring Donald Barthelme." *New York Times Book Review*, September 3, 1989, 9.

Barthelme, Donald. "Robert Kennedy Saved From Drowning." In *Unspeakable Practices, Unnatural Acts*. New York: Farrar Strauss & Giroux, 1968. 35-47.

Bechtel, Roger. *Past performance: American Theater and the Historical Imagination*. Lewisburg: Bucknell University Press, 2007.

Bergé, Carol. "Pavane for the White Queen." In *Of Poetry and Power: Poems Occasioned by the Presidency and by the Death of John F. Kennedy*. Edited by Erwin A. Glikes and Paul Schwaber. New York: Basic, 1964. 121.

Bernstein, Irving. *Promises Kept: John F. Kennedy's New Frontier*. New York, Oxford: Oxford University Press, 1991.

Berryman, John. "Formal Elegy." In *Of Poetry and Power: Poems Occasioned by the Presidency and by the Death of John F. Kennedy*. Edited by Erwin A. Glikes and Paul Schwaber. New York: Basic, 1964. 44-7.

Beschloss, Michael R. *The Crisis Years: Kennedy and Khrushev, 1960-1963*. New York: HarperCollins, 1991.

–, *Presidential Courage: Brave Leaders and How They Changed America, 1789-1989*. New York: Simon & Schuster, 2007.

Blackburn, Thomas. "*MacBird!* and *Macbeth*: Topicality and Imitation in Barbara Garson's Satirical Pastiche." In *Macbeth and Its Afterlife*. Edited by Peter Holland. Cambridge: Cambridge University Press, 2004. 137-44.

Blakey, Robert. *The Plot to Kill the President*. New York: New York Times Book, 1981.

Blight, James G. and David A. Welch, eds. *On the Brink: Americans and Soviets Reexamine the Cuban Missile Crisis*. New York: Hill &Wang, 1989.

Blight, James G., Bruce J. Allyn and David A. Welch. *Cuba on the Brink: The Missile Crisis and the Soviet Collapse*. New York: Rowman & Littlefield, 2002.

Bodnar, John. *The Transplanted: A History of Immigrants in Urban America*. Bloomington: Indiana University Press, 1985.

Bosmaijan, Hamida. "Robert Frost's 'The Gift Outright': Wish and Reality in History and Poetry." *American Quarterly* 22:1 (1970). 93-105.

Bourjaily, Vance. *The man who knew Kennedy*. [New York]: Dial Press, 1967.

Brackmann, Jacob. "Onward and Upward with the Arts." *The New Yorker*, June 24, 1967, 34-6, 70.

Bradlee, Benjamin C. *Conversations with Kennedy*. New York: Norton, 1975.

Brautigan, Richard. *The Tokyo-Montana Express*. London: Pan, 1980.

Brown, Thomas. *JFK: History of an Image*. Bloomington: Indiana University Press, 1988.

Buckley, William F. Jr. *See You Later Alligator*. London: Arrow, 1985.

–, *The Blackford Oakes Reader*. New York: toExcel, 1995.

–, *The Right Word*. New York: Harcort Brace & Co., 1996.

–, *Miles Gone by*. Washington, D.C.: Regnery, 2004.

Burner, David. *John F. Kennedy and a New Generation*. Boston: Little, Brown & Co., 1988.

C-Span 2009, Historians Presidential Leadership Survey. <http://www.c-span.org/PresidentialSurvey/Overall-Ranking.aspx> (March 15, 2010).

Caruth, Cathy. "Recapturing the Past: Introduction." In *Trauma: Explorations in Memory*. Edited by Cathy Caruth. Baltimore, London: Johns Hopkins University Press, 1995. 151-57.

Condon, Richard. *Winter Kills*. New York: Dell, [[1]1975] 1984.

Cook, Gareth. "The dark side of camp – analysis of camp style and society." *Washington Monthly*, September 1995. <http://findarticles.com/p/articles/mi_m1316/is_n9_v27/17292791> (September 15, 2010).

Cutler, Robert B. *Crossfire: Evidence of Conspiracy*. Danvers, Mass.: Bett's & Mirror Press, 1975.

Dallek, Robert. *An Unfinished Life: John F. Kennedy 1917-1963*. New York: Little, Brown & Co./ Back Bay, 2003.

Davis, John H. *Mafia Kingfish: Carlos Marcello and the Assassination of John F. Kennedy*. New York: New American Library, 1989.

–, *The Kennedy Contract: The Mafia Plot to Assassinate the President*. New York: Harper, 1993.

deCurtis, Anthony. "'An Outsider in This Society': An Interview With Don DeLillo." In *Conversations With Don DeLillo*. Edited by Thomas DePietro. Jackson: University Press of Mississippi, 2005. 52-74.

DeLillo, Don. *Americana*. London: Penguin, [[1]1971] 1989.

–, "American Blood: A Journey Through the Labyrinth of Dallas and JFK." *Rolling Stone*, December 8, 1983, 21-28, 74.

DeLillo, Don. *Libra.* London: Penguin, 1988.

Dickstein, Morris. *Gates of Eden: American Culture in the Sixties.* New York: Basic, 1977.

Douglass, James D. *JFK and the Unspeakable: Why He Died and Why It Matters.* New York: Orbis, 2008.

Ellroy, James. *American Tabloid.* London: Vintage, 2001.

Erll, Astrid. *Gedächtnisromane: Literatur über den Ersten Weltkrieg als Medium englischer und deutscher Erinnerungskulturen in den 1920er Jahren.* Trier: Wissenschaftlicher Verlag Trier, 2003.

–, "Kollektives Gedächtnis und Erinnerungskulturen." In: *Einführung in die Kulturwissenschaften.* Edited by Ansgar Nünning & Vera Nünning. Stuttgart: Metzler, 2008. 158-85.

Final Report of the Select Committee on Assassinations: Summary of Findings and Recommendations. January 2, 1979. Washington: Government Printing Office, 1979.

Fluck, Winfried. *Inszenierte Wirklichkeit: Der amerikanische Realismus, 1865-1890.* München: Fink, 1992.

Freese, Peter. "Donald Barthelmes *fictions*: Fragmente aus Wörtern mit Würmern." *Jahrbuch für Amerikastudien* 19 (1974), 126-141.

Frost, Robert. "The Gift Outright." In *Of Poetry and Power: Poems Occasioned by the Presidency and by the Death of John F. Kennedy.* Edited by Erwin A. Glikes and Paul Schwaber. New York: Basic, 1964. 10.

–, "For John F. Kennedy His Inauguration." In *Of Poetry and Power: Poems Occasioned by the Presidency and by the Death of John F. Kennedy.* Edited by Erwin A. Glikes and Paul Schwaber. New York: Basic, 1964.7-9.

Garson, Barbara. *MacBird!* Berkeley: Grassy Knoll Press, 1966.

Garthoff, Raymond L. "US Intelligence and the Cuban Missile Crisis." In *Intelligence and the Cuban Missile Crisis.* Edited by James G. Blight and David A. Welsh. London, Portland: Frank Cass, 1998. 18-63.

Gilbert, Robert E. "The Contemporary Presidency: The Twenty-Fifth Amendment: Recommendations and Deliberations of the Working Group on Presidential Disability." *Presidential Studies Quarterly* 33:4 (2003), 877-88.

Ginsberg, Allen. "When the Mode of the Music Changes, the Walls of the City Shake." In *Deliberate Prose: Selected Essays 1952-1999 – Allen Ginsberg.* Edited by Bill Morgan. New York: HarperCollins, 2000. 247-53.

–, "Reflections on the Mantra." In *Deliberate Prose: Selected Essays 1952-1999 – Allen Ginsberg.* Edited by Bill Morgan. New York: HarperCollins, 2000. 148-50.

–, "Nov. 23, 1963: Alone." *Collected Poems 1947-1997.* New York, London: Penguin, 2009. 341-2.

Goldberg , Peter. "Kennedy Remembered." *Newsweek*, November 28, 1983, 33-6.
Goldstein, William. "PW Interviews: Don DeLillo." In *Conversations with Don DeLillo*. Edited by Thomas dePietro. Jackson: University Press of Mississippi, 2005. 47-51.
Goodwin, Doris Kearns. *The Fitzgeralds and the Kennedys*. New York: St. Martin's Press, 1987
Goodwin, Richard N. to JFK. "Memorandum from the President's Special Counsel (Goodwin) to President Kennedy." Washington, August 22, 1961. *Foreign Relations of the United States*. 1961-1963. Vol. X. Washington: United States Government Printing Office, 1997. Kennedy Administration Volumes, Cuba 1961-1962. Documents and Memoranda Series. 256 <http://www.state.gov/www/about state/history/frusX/256-70.index.html> (June 23, 2011).
Goodwin, Richard N. *Remembering America: A Voice from the Sixties*. New York: Harper & Row, 1988.
Gordon, Lois. *Donald Barthelme*. Boston: Twayne, 1981.
Graubard, Stephen. *The Presidents: The Transformation of the American Presidency from Theodore Roosevelt to George W. Bush*. New York, London: Penguin, 2004.
Griffith, Nancy. "It's a Hard Life Wherever You Go." Emmylou Harris and the Nash Ramblers. *At the Ryman*. [CD] Reprise, 1992.
Großmann, Claudia. *Richard Brautigan. Pounding at the Gates of American Literature: Untersuchungen zu seiner Lyrik und Prosa*. Heidelberg: Carl Winter, Universitätsverlag, 1986.
Hamilton, Nigel. *Life and Death of an American President, Vol I: Reckless Youth*. London: Century, 1992.
Harper, Paul and Joann B. Krieg, eds. *John F. Kennedy: The Promise Revisited*. New York: Greenwood Press, 1988.
Harris, Louis. *The Anguish of Change*. New York: Norton, 1973.
Hartsock, John C. "'Literary Journalism' as an Epistemological Moving Object within a Larger 'Quantum' Narrative." *Journal of Communication Inquiry* 23:4 (1999), 432-47.
Hellmann, John. *The Kennedy Obsession: The American Myth of JFK*. New York: Columbia University Press, 1997.
Hicks, Walter Jackson. *An Essay on Recent American Fiction*. Chapel Hill: University of North Carolina Press, 1974.
Hicks, Jack. *In the Singer's Temple: Prose Fictions of Barthelme, Gaines, Brautigan, Piercy, Kesey, and Kosinski*. Chapel Hill: University of North Carolina Press, 1981.
Hilsman, Roger. *The Cuban Missile Crisis: The Struggle Over Policy*. Westport, Conn.: Praeger, 1996.

Hoffer, Peter Charles. “Kennedy and the Regeneration of America.” In *John F. Kennedy: Person, Policy, Presidency.* Edited by J. Richard Snyder. Wilmington, Del.: SR, 1988. 35-43.

Holler, Robert, “Abraham, Martin and John.” Emmylou Harris and the Nash Ramblers. *At the Ryman*. [CD] Reprise, 1992.

Houchin, John H. *Censorship of the American Theatre in the Twentieth Century.* New York, Cambridge: Cambridge University Press, 2003.

“How to lead in a dangerous world.” *Time,* July 2, 2007, cover.

Howard, Gerald, ed. *The Sixties.* New York: Washington Square Press, 1982.

Huismann, Wilfried. *Rendezvous mit dem Tod: Warum John F. Kennedy sterben musste*. Munich: Pendo, 2006.

Hutcheon, Linda. *A Poetics of Postmodernism.* New York, London: Routledge, 1988.

–, *The Politics of Postmodernism*. New York: Routledge, 1989.

“Intimations of Mortality.” *Time,* February 10, 1967. <http://time.com/time/magazine/article/0,9171,840865-2,00.html> (July 29, 2010).

Janet, Pierre. *L'automatisme Psychologique: Essai de Psychologie Expérimentale sur les Formes Inférieures de L'activité Humaine*. Paris: Alcan, 1894 .

Kane, John. “American Values or Human Rights? U.S. Foreign Policy and the Fractured Myth of Virtuous Power.” *Presidential Studies Quarterly* 33:4 (2003), 772-800.

Kanfer, Stefan. “Fly on the Wall: ‘See You Later Alligator’.” *Time*, February 4, 1985. 74.

Kennedy, Edward M. *True Compass.* [London]: Little, Brown & Co., 2009.

Kennedy, John F. *Profiles in Courage*. New York: Harper, [[1]1955] 2003.

–, “Nomination Acceptance Speech.” Los Angeles, Cal., July 15, 1960. In *Let the Word Go Forth: The Speeches, Statements, and Writings of John F. Kennedy.* Edited by Theodore C. Sorensen. New York: Delacorte Press, 1988. 96-102.

–, *The Strategy of Peace*. Edited by Allan Nevins. New York: Harper & Row, 1960.

–, “Opening Statement, First Televised Presidential Candidates Debate.” Chicago, Ill., September 26, 1960. In *Let the Word Go Forth: The Speeches, Statements, and Writings of John F. Kennedy.* Edited by Theodore C. Sorensen. New York: Delacorte Press, 1988. 103-5.

–, “Inaugural Address”. Washington, D.C., January 20, 1961. In *Let the Word Go Forth: The Speeches, Statements, and Writings of John F. Kennedy.* Edited by Theodore C. Sorensen. New York: Delacorte Press, 1988, 12-5.

–, “Televised Address on Berlin Crisis.” Washington, D.C., July 25, 1961. In *Let the Word Go Forth: The Speeches, Statements, and Writings of John F. Kennedy.* Edited by Theodore C. Sorensen. New York: Delacorte Press, 1988. 257-63.

Kennedy, John F. "American University Address." Washington, D.C., June 10, 1963. In *Let the Word Go Forth: The Speeches, Statements, and Writings of John F. Kennedy.* Edited by Theodore C. Sorensen. New York: Delacorte Press, 1988. 282-90.

Kennedy, Robert F. *Thirteen Days: A Memoir of the Cuban Missile Crisis.* New York: Norton, [1 1968] 1971.

–, *To Seek a Newer World.* New York: Bantam, 1967.

"Kennedy has Become America's Favorite President." *Newsweek*, November 28, 1983. 36.

"The Kennedy Legacy." *Newsweek*, November 28, 1983, 38.

Kifner, John. "The Nation – Once More, With Feeling: Recycling the Kennedys." *The New York Times*, November 16, 1997, 4.

King, Stephen. *11.22.63.* London: Hodder & Stoughton, 2011.

Kissinger, Henry. *Diplomacy.* New York: Simon & Schuster, 1994.

Krim, Seymour. *Shake it for the world.* London: Allison & Busby, 1971.

Lane, Mark. *Plausible Denial: Was the CIA Involved in the Assassination of JFK?* London: Plexus, 1988

Lathem, Edward C., ed. *Interviews with Robert Frost.* Guildford, Conn.: Jeffrey Norton, 1997.

Leamer, Lawrence. *The Kennedy Men.* New York: HarperCollins, 2001.

"The Legacy of JFK: Reflections on the President, the Man and the Myth." *Newsweek*, November 28, 1983, 37.

Leuchtenburg, William E. "Kennedy and a New Generation." In *John F. Kennedy: Person, Policy, Presidency.* Edited by J. Richard Snyder. Wilmington, Del.: SR, 1988. 11-24.

Lenz, Bernd. *Factifiction: Agentenspiele wie in der Realität: Wirklichkeitsanspruch und Wirklichkeitsgehalt des Agentenromans.* Heidelberg: Carl Winter, Universitätsverlag, 1987.

Lerner, Alan Jay and Frederick Loewe. "Finale Ultimo." *Camelot.* Motion Picture Soundtrack. [CD]Warner Brothers Records, 1968.

Lifton, David. *Best Evidence.* New York: Macmillan, 1980.

Lipset, Seymour Martin. *American Exceptionalism: A Double-Edged Sword.* New York: Norton, 1996.

Little, Robert. *The Sisters.* New York: Bantam, 1986.

MacLeod, Wendy. *The House of Yes.* New York: Dramatists Play Service, 1996.

Mailer, Norman. *The Presidential Papers.* Frogmore: Panther, [1 1964] 1977.

–, *The Armies of the Night: History as a Novel – The Novel as History.* New York: Plume, 1968.

–, *An American Dream.* London: Panther, 1972.

–, *Harlot's Ghost.* New York: Random House, 1991.

Manchester, William. *Portrait of a President: John F. Kennedy in Profile*. Boston: Little, Brown & Co., 1962.

–, *The Death of a President*. New York: Harper & Row, 1967.

–, *Controversy and other essays in journalism, 1950-1975*. London: Little, Brown & Co., 1976.

Marrs, Jim. *Crossfire: The Plot that Killed Kennedy*. New York: Carrol & Graf, 1989.

May, Ernest R. & Philip D. Zelikow, eds. *The Kennedy Tapes: Inside the White House during the Cuban Missile Crisis*. Cambridge: The Belknap Press of Harvard University Press, 1997.

Mazlish, Bruce. "Kennedy: Myth and History." In *John F. Kennedy: Person, Policy, Presidency*. Edited by J. Richard Snyder. Wilmington, Del.: SR, 1988. 25-34.

McCaffery, Larry. *Postmodern Fiction*. New York: Greenwood Press, 1986.

McCarry, Charles. *The Tears of Autumn*. New York: Signet, 1974.

McNamara, Robert S. *In Retrospect*. New York: Time Books Random House, 1995.

Meagher, Sylvia. *Accessories After the Fact*. New York: Vintage, 1976.

Mitgang, Herbert. "Behind the Bestsellers: Anton Myrer." *The New York Times Book Review*, May 28, 1978, 6.

Morris, Edmund. *Dutch: A Memoir of Ronald Reagan*. New York: Random House, 1999.

Morris, Wright. *One Day*. Lincoln, London: University of Nebraska Press, 1965.

Myrer, Anton. *The Last Convertible*. New York: Berkley, 1979.

Nasaw, David. *The Patriarch: The Remarkable Life and Turbulent Times of Joseph P. Kennedy*. New York: Penguin Press, 2012.

Nielsen, Heather. "Jack's Ghost: Reappearances of John F. Kennedy in the Work of Gore Vidal and Norman Mailer." *American Studies International* 35:3 (1997), 23-41.

O'Brien, Michael. *John F. Kennedy: A Biography*. New York: St. Martin's Press, 2005.

O'Donnell, Kenneth P., David F. Powers, and Joe McCarthy. "*Johnny, We Hardly Knew Ye*": *Memories of John Fitzgerald Kennedy*. New York: Kangaroo, 1972.

Oates, Joyce Carol. "The Union Justified the Means." *The New York Times Book Review*, June 3, 1984, 1.

–, "Updike's American Comedies." In *John Updike*. Edited by Harald Bloom. Modern Critical Views. Philadelphia: Chelsea House, 1986. 57-68.

Parmet, Herbert S. *Jack: The Struggles of John F. Kennedy*. New York: Dial Press, 1980.

–, *JFK: The Presidency of John F. Kennedy*. Harmondsworth: Penguin, 1984.

Piereson, James. *Camelot and the Cultural Revolution*. New York: Encounter, 2007.

Pizer, Donald. "Documentary Narrative as Art: William Manchester and Truman Capote." In *The Reporter as Artist: A Look at the New Journalism Controversy*. Edited by Ronald Weber. New York: Hastings House, 1974. 207-19.

Posner, Gerald. *Case Closed: Lee Harvey Oswald and the Assassination of JFK*. New York: Random House, 1993.

Prouty, L. Fletcher. *JFK: The CIA, Vietnam, and the Plot to Assassinate John F. Kennedy*. New York: Skyhorse, 2009.

Ragano, Frank and Selwyn Raab. *Mob Lawyer*. [New York]: Charles Scribner's Sons: 1994.

Rampton, David. "Plexed Artistry: The Formal Case for *Harlot's Ghost*." *Journal of Modern Literature* 30:1 (2006): 47-61.

Reed, Lou. "The Day John Kennedy Died". *The Blue Mask*. [CD] BMG Entertainment International, [[1]1982] 1999.

Reeves, Richard. *President Kennedy: Profile of Power*. New York: Simon & Schuster, 1993.

Reeves, Thomas C. *A Question of Character: A Life of John F. Kennedy*. New York: Free Press, 1991.

Renauld, Mary. *The King Must Die*. New York, London: Bantam, [[1]1958] 1972.

Report of the Select Committee on Assassinations: Findings and Recommendations. March 29, 1979. Washington: Government Printing Office, 1979.

Reston, James. "The Problems to Come: Kennedy's Solution to Problems May Prove Radical in Long Run." *The New York Times*, January 20, 1961, 1.

Robert Rauschenberg: Im Gespräch mit Barbara Rose. Cologne: Kiepenheuer & Witsch, 1989.

Rorabaugh, W.J. *Kennedy and the Promise of the Sixties*. Cambridge: Cambridge University Press, 2002.

Saad, Lydia. "JFK and Ronald Reagan Win Gallup Presidents Day Poll." *Gallup News Service,* February 18, 2008 <http://www.gallup.com/poll/104380/JFK-Ronald-Reagan-Win-Gallup-Presidents-Day-Poll.aspx> (June 3, 2009).

Schabert, Ina. *Der historische Roman in England und Amerika*. Darmstadt: Wissenschaftliche Buchgesellschaft, 1981.

Scheim, David. *Contract on America*: *The Mafia Murder of President John F. Kennedy*. New York: Zebra, 1989.

Schlesinger, Arthur Jr.. *A Thousand Days: John F. Kennedy in the White House*. Greenwich, Conn.: Fawcett, 1965.

–, *Robert Kennedy and His Times*. New York: Ballantine, 1978.

–, "Camelot Revisited." *The New Yorker*, June 5, 1995, 33.

Scott, Peter D. *Deep Politics and the Death of JFK*. Berkeley: University of California Press, 1993.

Shapiro, Harvey. "The Story of a Poem." *The New York Times Magazine*, January 15, 1961, 6.

Sheed, Wilfrid. "Armaggedon Now?" *The New York Review of Books*, December 5, 1991. <http://nybooks.com/article/articles-preview> (June 20, 2010).

Simon, John. "The Company They Keep." *The York Times Sunday Review of Books*, September 29, 1991, 26.

Sontag, Susan. "Notes on 'Camp'." In *Against Interpretation and other Essays*. New York: Picador, 1966. 275-92.

Sorensen, Ted. *Counselor: A Life at the Edge of History*. New York: HarperCollins, 2008.

Stengel, Wayne. *The Shape of the Art in the Short Stories of Donald Barthelme*. Baton Rouge: Louisiana State University Press, 1985.

Stevenson, David L. "What Was It Like to Be Oneself?" *The New York Times*, March 7, 1963, 32.

Sweatt, Susanne M. *Postmodernism in the Fiction of Richard Brautigan*. Diss., Middle Tennessee State University. 1985.

Szulc, Tad. "Modernized Army Called Cuba's Aim". *The New York Times*, September 3, 1962, 2.

Talbot, David. "Warrior for Peace". *Time*, June 2, 2007, 45-50.

–, *Brothers: The Hidden History of the Kennedy Years*. New York: Pocket, 2007.

Tanner, Tony. "A Compromised Environment." In *John Updike*. Edited by Harold Bloom. Modern Critical Views. Philadelphia: Chelsea House, 1986. 37-56.

Thomas, Glen. "History, Biography, and Narrative in Don DeLillo's *Libra*." *Twentieth Century Literature* 43:1 (1997), 106-24.

Thompson, Robert Smith. *The Missiles of October: The Declassified Story of John F. Kennedy and the Cuban Missile Crisis*. New York: Simon & Schuster, 1992.

Tricomi, Albert H. *Reading Tudor-Stuart Texts Through Cultural Historicism*. Gainesville: University Press of Florida, 1996.

Tyler, Anne. "Dallas Echoing Down the Decades." *New York Times*, July 24, 1988. <chttp://www.nytimes.com/books/97/03/16/lifetimes/del-r-libra.html?> (November 19, 2010).

Uellenberg, Klaus. "Postmodern American Short Fiction: Donald Barthelme, Richard Brautigan – Fractal Attraction." *Recent American Short Story Writing* (*a&e* 44). Heidelberg: Carl Winter, Universitätsverlag, 1991. 121-46.

Updike, John. *Couples*. Harmondsworth: Penguin, 1968.

Waldron, Lamar and Thom Hartmann. *Legacy of Secrecy: The Long Shadow of the JFK Assassination*. Berkeley: Counterpoint, 2009.

Van der Kolk, Bessel and Onno van der Hart. "The Intrusive Past: The Flexibility of Memory and the Engraving of Trauma." In *Trauma: Explorations in Memory*. Edited by Cathy Caruth. Baltimore: Johns Hopkins University Press, 1995. 158-82.

"Vergnügen mit Hexen." *Der Spiegel*, February 27, 1967, 122.

White, Mark J. *The Cuban Missile Crisis*. Houndmills, London: Macmillan Press, 1996.

White, Theodore H. *The Making of the President 1960*. New York: Mentor, [[1]1961] 1967.

Wills, Gary. *The Kennedy Imprisonment: A Meditation on Power*. New York: Pocket, 1981.

Winthrop, John. "A Model of Christian Charity" <http://religiousfreedom.lib.virginia.edusacred/charity.html> (October 13, 2008).

Wydeven, Joseph J. *Wright Morris Revisited*. New York: Twayne, 1998.

Zelizer, Barbie. *Covering the Body: The Kennedy Assassination, the Media, and the Shaping of Collective Memory*. Chicago: University of Chicago Press, 1992.

Sing about Mahatma Ghandi
Sing of Martin Luther King
Sing of Jesus Christ Almighty
And the brothers Kennedy

Kris Kristofferson,
"They Killed Him"